Intelligence, Surveillance, and Reconnaissance: DOD Can Better Assess and Integrate ISR Capabilities and Oversee Development of Future ISR Requirements

United States Government Accountability Office

United States Government Accountability Office

GAO

Report to the Subcommittee on Air and Land Forces, Committee on Armed Services, House of Representatives

March 2008

INTELLIGENCE, SURVEILLANCE, AND RECONNAISSANCE

DOD Can Better Assess and Integrate ISR Capabilities and Oversee Development of Future ISR Requirements

G A O

Accountability ★ Integrity ★ Reliability

INTELLIGENCE, SURVEILLANCE, AND RECONNAISSANCE

DOD Can Better Assess and Integrate ISR Capabilities and Oversee Development of Future ISR Requirements

Highlights of GAO-08-374, a report to Subcommittee on Air and Land Forces, Committee on Armed Services, House of Representatives

Why GAO Did This Study

The Department of Defense's (DOD) intelligence, surveillance, and reconnaissance (ISR) capabilities–such as satellites and unmanned aircraft systems–are crucial to military operations, and demand for ISR capabilities has increased. For example, DOD plans to invest $28 billion over the next 7 years in 20 airborne ISR systems alone. Congress directed DOD to fully integrate its ISR capabilities, also known as the ISR enterprise, as it works to meet current and future ISR needs. GAO was asked to (1) describe the challenges, if any, that DOD faces in integrating its ISR enterprise, (2) assess DOD's management approach for improving integration of its future ISR investments, and (3) evaluate the extent to which DOD has implemented key activities to ensure proposed new ISR capabilities fill gaps, are not duplicative, and use a joint approach to meeting warfighters' needs. GAO assessed DOD's integration initiatives and 19 proposals for new ISR capabilities. We supplemented this analysis with discussions with DOD officials.

What GAO Recommends

GAO recommends that DOD develop a future ISR enterprise vision and that DOD take steps to improve its process for identifying future ISR capabilities. DOD agreed or partially agreed with some recommendations but disagreed with the recommendation to review staffing levels needed for key oversight activities.

To view the full product, including the scope and methodology, click on GAO-08-374. For more information, contact Davi M. D'Agostino at (202) 512-5431 or dagostinod@gao.gov.

What GAO Found

DOD faces a complex and challenging environment in supporting defense requirements for ISR capabilities as well as national intelligence efforts. Past efforts to improve integration across DOD and national intelligence agencies have been hampered by the diverse missions and different institutional cultures of the many intelligence agencies that DOD supports. For example, DOD had difficulty obtaining complete information on national ISR assets that could support military operations because of security classifications of other agency documents. Further, different funding arrangements for defense and national intelligence activities complicate integration of interagency activities. While DOD develops the defense intelligence budget, some DOD activities also receive funding through the national intelligence budget to provide support for national intelligence efforts. Disagreements about equitable funding from each budget have led to program delays. Separate military and intelligence requirements identification processes also complicate efforts to integrate future ISR investments.

DOD does not have a clearly defined vision of a future ISR enterprise to guide its ISR investments. DOD has taken a significant step toward integrating its ISR activities by developing an ISR Integration Roadmap that includes existing and currently planned ISR systems. However, the Roadmap does not provide long-term view of what capabilities are required to achieve strategic goals or provide detailed information that would make it useful as a basis for deciding among alternative investments. Without a clear vision of the desired ISR end state and sufficient detail on existing and planned systems, DOD decision makers lack a basis for determining where additional capabilities are required prioritizing investments, or assessing progress in achieving strategic goals, as well as identifying areas where further investment may not be warranted.

DOD policy calls for the services and agencies that sponsor proposals for new ISR capabilities to conduct comprehensive assessments of current and planned ISR systems, but GAO's review of 19 proposals showed that 12 sponsors did not complete assessments, and the completeness of the remaining 7 sponsors' assessments varied. GAO found that the DOD board charged with reviewing ISR proposals did not consistently coordinate with sponsors to ensure the quality of the assessments supporting their proposals or review the completed assessments. There were three key reasons for this. First, the board did not have a comprehensive, readily available source of information about existing and developmental ISR capabilities that could help identify alternatives to new systems. Second, the board has no monitoring mechanism to ensure that key activities are fully implemented. Third, DOD board officials said that the board lacks adequate numbers of dedicated, skilled personnel to engage in early coordination with sponsors and to review sponsors' assessments. Without more complete information on alternatives and a monitoring mechanism to ensure these key activities are fully implemented, DOD is not in the best position to ensure that investment decisions are consistent with departmentwide priorities.

_____ United States Government Accountability Offi

Contents

Abbreviations

BA FCB	Battlespace Awareness Functional Capabilities Board
DOD	Department of Defense
FAA	Functional Area Analysis
FNA	Functional Needs Analysis
FSA	Functional Solution Analysis
ISR	Intelligence, Surveillance, and Reconnaissance
JCIDS	Joint Capabilities Integration and Development System
MIP	Military Intelligence Program
NIP	National Intelligence Program
USD(I)	Under Secretary of Defense for Intelligence

March 24, 2008

The Honorable Neil Abercrombie
Chairman
The Honorable Jim Saxton
Ranking Member
Subcommittee on Air and Land Forces
Committee on Armed Services
House of Representatives

The Department of Defense's (DOD) intelligence, surveillance, and reconnaissance (ISR) systems—including manned and unmanned airborne, space-borne, maritime, and terrestrial systems—play critical roles in supporting military operations and national security missions. ISR encompasses multiple activities related to the planning and operation of systems that collect, process, and disseminate data in support of current and future military operations. Examples of these ISR systems include surveillance and reconnaissance systems ranging from satellites, to manned aircraft such as the U-2, to unmanned aircraft systems such as the Air Force's Global Hawk and Predator and the Army's Hunter, to other ground-, air-, sea-, or space-based equipment, and to human intelligence teams. The intelligence data provided by these ISR systems can take many forms, including optical, radar, or infrared images or electronic signals. Effective ISR data can provide early warning of enemy threats as well as enable U.S. military forces to increase effectiveness, coordination, and lethality, and demand for ISR capabilities to support ongoing military operations has increased. To meet this growing demand, DOD is planning to make sizeable investments in ISR systems, which provide ISR capabilities. For example, over the next 7 years, DOD plans to invest over $28 billion to develop, procure, and modify 20 major airborne ISR systems alone, and maintain existing systems until new ones are fielded. These investments are planned at a time when, as we have previously reported, the nation is facing significant fiscal challenges in the future, due primarily to demographic changes and rising health care costs, which are expected to increase downward pressure on all federal spending, including defense spending. [1] In this environment, it will be increasingly important for DOD

---

[1] GAO, *Federal Financial Management: Critical Accountability and Fiscal Stewardship Challenges Facing Our Nation*, GAO-07-542T (Washington, D.C.: Mar. 1, 2007); and *Fiscal and Retirement Challenges*, GAO-07-1263CG (New York: Sep. 19, 2007).

decision makers to evaluate competing priorities and alternatives to determine the most cost-effective solutions for providing needed capabilities, including ISR capabilities. The Senate Armed Services Committee has stated concerns that the effectiveness of United States ISR capabilities has been hampered by capability gaps as well as parallel systems across the services and intelligence agencies that do not fully complement one another and may duplicate some capabilities. For this reason, the Committee has expressed a question about whether enough has been done, in a comprehensive, defensewide enterprise manner, to require that new intelligence capabilities being developed by the military services and the defense intelligence agencies be conceived as part of a larger system of systems.

The National Defense Authorization Act for Fiscal Year 2004 states that it shall be a goal of DOD to fully integrate the ISR capabilities and coordinate the developmental activities of the services, DOD intelligence agencies, and combatant commands as they work to meet current and future ISR needs.[2] Moreover, the position of the Under Secretary of Defense for Intelligence (USD(I)) was established to facilitate resolution of the challenges to achieving an integrated DOD ISR structure. Within DOD, USD(I) exercises policy and strategic oversight over all defense intelligence, counterintelligence, and security plans and programs, including ISR. As part of this responsibility, USD(I) manages ISR capabilities across the department, as well as DOD's intelligence budget, which includes DOD spending on ISR. USD(I) carries out these responsibilities within the context of the department's resource allocation process, known as the Planning, Programming, Budgeting, and Execution process. DOD's ISR capabilities are often referred to as DOD's ISR enterprise, which consists of DOD intelligence organizations that operate ISR systems that collect, process, and disseminate ISR data in order to meet defense intelligence needs, as well as to meet a significant set of U.S. governmentwide intelligence needs, as tasked by the Director of National Intelligence.[3]

---

[2] Pub. L. No. 108-136, § 923(b), codified at 10 U.S.C. § 426 note.

[3] The Intelligence Reform and Terrorism Prevention Act of 2004 (P.L. 108-458) created a Director of National Intelligence to head the U.S. intelligence community, serve as the principal intelligence adviser to the President, and oversee and direct the acquisition of major collections systems. The U.S. intelligence community is a federation of 16 different defense and non-defense intelligence agencies that carries out intelligence activities necessary for the conduct of foreign relations and the protection of national security.

DOD implemented the Joint Capabilities Integration and Development System (JCIDS) in 2003 as the department's principal process for identifying, assessing, and prioritizing joint military capabilities.[4] JCIDS supports the Chairman of the Joint Chiefs of Staff, who is responsible for advising the Secretary of Defense on the priorities of military requirements in support of the national military strategy. The Joint Requirements Oversight Council[5] assists the Chairman in this role by reviewing and approving proposals for new military capabilities, among other responsibilities.[6] The Joint Requirements Oversight Council is supported by eight Functional Capabilities Boards that review and analyze initial proposals for new military capabilities. The Functional Capabilities Board responsible for reviewing proposals for new ISR capabilities is known as the Battlespace Awareness Functional Capabilities Board (BA FCB).[7] Proposals for new military capabilities may be developed by any of the military services, defense agencies, or combatant commands, who are referred to as sponsors. To support these proposals and to facilitate the development of capabilities that are as joint and efficient as possible, Joint Staff policy calls for the sponsors to conduct capabilities-based assessments that identify gaps in military capabilities and potential solutions for filling those gaps. Specifically, the capabilities-based assessment identifies the capabilities required to successfully execute missions, the shortfalls in existing systems to deliver those capabilities, and the possible solutions for the capability shortfalls.

We conducted several reviews in 2007 related to DOD's management of its ISR capabilities. In April 2007, we testified that, although DOD is

---

[4] JCIDS is a deliberate process designed for addressing future needs, but DOD has other sources for identifying capability needs, including Joint Urgent Operational Needs for immediate needs, combatant commanders' integrated priority lists, lessons learned, and transitioning improvised explosive device initiatives. However, complying with the JCIDS process is required for the long-term solution, sustainment activities, or to transition the solution into a program of record.

[5] The Joint Requirements Oversight Council consists of the Vice Chairman of the Joint Chiefs of Staff and a four-star officer designated by each of the military services.

[6] Joint Staff policy describes the documentation developed during the JCIDS process as including an Initial Capabilities Document, which documents the results of a capabilities-based assessment. For the purposes of this report, we use the phrase "proposals for new military capabilities" to refer to Initial Capabilities Documents. More specifically, we use the phrase "proposals for new ISR capabilities" to refer to ISR-related Initial Capabilities Documents.

[7] The other Functional Capabilities Boards are Command and Control, Focused Logistics, Force Management, Force Protection, Force Application, Net-Centric, and Joint Training.

undertaking some initiatives to set strategic goals and improve integration of ISR assets, it has not comprehensively identified future ISR requirements, set funding priorities, or established mechanisms to measure progress.[8] We also testified that DOD did not have efficient processes for maximizing the capabilities of its current and planned unmanned aircraft systems or measuring their effectiveness. Furthermore, we reported that acquisition of ISR systems continued to suffer from cost increases or schedule delays, and we noted opportunities to improve ISR acquisition outcomes through greater synergies among various ISR platforms. In May 2007, we reported on DOD's acquisition of ISR systems and made recommendations to improve acquisition outcomes by developing and implementing an integrated, enterprise-level investment strategy approach based on a joint assessment of warfighting needs and a full set of potential and viable alternative solutions, considering cross-service solutions including new acquisitions and modifications to legacy systems within realistic and affordable budget projections.[9] In July 2007, we issued a report on DOD's processes for using unmanned aircraft systems that made recommendations to improve visibility over and the coordination of those assets and to measure their effectiveness.[10] In addition, we are currently conducting a separate review of the JCIDS process that addresses the extent to which the process has improved outcomes in weapons system acquisition programs. We expect our report based on this review to be issued later in 2008.

In response to your request, our objectives for this report were to (1) describe the challenges, if any, that DOD faces in achieving an integrated ISR enterprise; (2) assess DOD's management approach for improving integration of its future ISR investments; and (3) evaluate the extent to which DOD has implemented key activities within the JCIDS process to ensure that proposed new ISR capabilities fill gaps, are not duplicative, and use a joint approach to filling warfighters' needs.

---

[8] GAO, *Intelligence, Surveillance, and Reconnaissance: Preliminary Observations on DOD's Approach to Managing Requirements for New Systems, Existing Assets, and Systems Development*, GAO-07-596T (Washington, D.C.: Apr. 19, 2007).

[9] GAO, *Defense Acquisitions: Greater Synergies Possible for DOD's Intelligence, Surveillance, and Reconnaissance Systems*, GAO-07-578 (Washington, D.C.: May 17, 2007).

[10] GAO, *Unmanned Aircraft Systems: Advanced Coordination and Increased Visibility Needed to Optimize Capabilities*, GAO-07-836 (Washington, D.C.: July 11, 2007).

To describe the challenges DOD faces in integrating its ISR enterprise, we reviewed documents on the operation of DOD's ISR enterprise and the national intelligence community. To assess DOD's management approach for improving integration of future ISR investments, we reviewed and analyzed DOD's ISR Integration Roadmap and other DOD ISR integration efforts and evaluated them against best practices for enterprise architecture and portfolio management. To assess the extent to which DOD has implemented key activities within the JCIDS process, we reviewed policies and procedures related to the review and approval of proposals for new ISR capabilities through DOD's JCIDS. We reviewed 19 of the 20 proposals for new ISR capabilities that were submitted to the Joint Staff since the implementation of JCIDS in 2003 and for which the BA FCB was designated as the primary Functional Capabilities Board.[11] We focused our efforts on the capabilities-based assessments that underpin these proposals by evaluating the extent to which the capabilities-based assessments incorporated key elements of Joint Staff policy and guidance. We discussed ISR-related efforts and challenges concerning these objectives with officials from such offices as the Office of the USD(I); Joint Staff; National Security Space Office; Air Force; Army; Navy; Marine Corps; U.S. Strategic Command's Joint Functional Component Command for ISR; U.S. Special Operations Command; U.S. Joint Forces Command; Defense Intelligence Agency; National Geospatial-Intelligence Agency; National Security Agency; and the Office of the Director of National Intelligence. We did not review other processes within DOD that may be used for rapidly identifying ISR capability needs, such as Joint Urgent Operational Needs, the Joint Rapid Acquisition Cell, and Joint Improvised Explosive Device Defeat Organization initiatives.

We conducted our review from April 2007 through March 2008 in accordance with generally accepted government auditing standards. More detailed information on our scope and methodology is provided in appendix I.

Results in Brief

As DOD works to achieve an integrated ISR enterprise, the department faces a complex and challenging environment in supporting a wide range of defense and non-defense agencies across the U.S. intelligence community. DOD is presented with different and sometimes competing

---

[11] We were unable to review one proposal for a new ISR capability because of the high classification level of this document.

organizational cultures, funding arrangements, and requirements processes, reflecting diverse missions across the many U.S. intelligence community agencies that DOD supports. For example, the Commission to Assess United States National Security Space Management and Organization noted in 2001 that understanding the different organizational cultures of the defense and national space communities is important for achieving long-term integration of defense and non-defense national security space activities—which are subset of ISR activities. In response to a commission recommendation, DOD established the National Security Space Office in 2003, which received funding and personnel from both DOD and the National Reconnaissance Office, a defense intelligence agency that develops overhead reconnaissance satellites for both DOD and the national intelligence community. However, in 2005, the National Reconnaissance Office withdrew its personnel, funding, and full access to a classified information-sharing network from the office, inhibiting efforts to integrate defense and national space activities, including ISR activities. Further, different funding arrangements for defense and national intelligence activities may complicate DOD's efforts to integrate ISR activities across the enterprise. While DOD develops the defense intelligence budget, some DOD organizations also receive funding through the national intelligence budget, which is developed by the Office of the Director of National Intelligence, to provide support for national intelligence efforts. However, statutorily required guidelines on how the Director of National Intelligence is to implement his authorities, including budgetary authority over defense intelligence agencies, have not yet been established. Disagreement about equitable funding from each budget may have led to at least one program delay until agreement could be reached. In addition, DOD and the Office of the Director of National Intelligence maintain separate processes for identifying future ISR requirements. This may complicate DOD efforts to develop future ISR systems that provide capabilities across the defense and national intelligence communities.

DOD has initiatives underway to improve the integration of its ISR investments; however, DOD lacks key management tools needed to ensure that ISR investments reflect enterprisewide priorities and strategic goals. DOD's two primary ISR integration initiatives—the ISR Integration Roadmap and a test case for managing ISR investments as a departmentwide portfolio—are positive steps toward managing ISR investments from an enterprise-level perspective rather than from a service or agency perspective. However, our previous work has shown that large organizations such as the DOD ISR enterprise are most successful when they employ the following key tools: (1) a clearly defined vision of a future enterprise that lays out what investments are needed to achieve strategic goals, and (2) a unified investment management approach in which decision makers weigh the relative costs, benefits, and risks of proposed investments using established criteria and methods. DOD and federal guidance on enterprise architecture also state that a framework for achieving an integrated enterprise should include these key tools. Although Congress tasked DOD to develop an ISR Integration Roadmap to guide the development and integration of DOD ISR capabilities from 2004 through 2018, USD(I) limited the Roadmap to articulating ISR programs already in DOD's 5-year ISR budget due to difficulty in predicting longer-term threats and mission requirements. As a result, the Roadmap does not provide a longer-term, comprehensive vision of what ISR capabilities are required to achieve strategic goals. Moreover, the Roadmap does not provide a sufficient level of detail to allow ISR decision makers to prioritize different needs and assess progress in achieving strategic goals. This lack of detail in the Roadmap limits its usefulness to ISR portfolio managers because it cannot serve as a basis for establishing criteria and a methodology that ISR decision makers can use to assess different ISR investments to identify the best return on investment in light of strategic goals. Without these two key tools, senior DOD leaders are not well-positioned to exert discipline over ISR spending. We are therefore recommending that the Secretary of Defense direct the USD(I) to develop and document a long-term, comprehensive vision of a future ISR enterprise that can serve as basis for prioritizing ISR needs and assessing how different investments contribute to achieving strategic goals.

DOD has not implemented key activities within the JCIDS process to ensure that proposed new ISR capabilities are filling gaps, are not duplicative, and use a joint approach to addressing warfighters' needs. Our review of the 19 proposals for new ISR capabilities submitted to the BA FCB by the military services and DOD agencies, also known as sponsors, since 2003 showed that sponsors did not consistently conduct comprehensive capabilities-based assessments as called for by Joint Staff policy, and the BA FCB did not fully conduct key oversight activities. Specifically, 12 sponsors did not complete the assessments, and the assessments conducted by the remaining 7 sponsors varied in completeness and rigor. Moreover, we found that the BA FCB did not systematically coordinate with the sponsors during their assessment process to help ensure the quality of the assessments, and did not generally review the assessments once they were completed. As a result, DOD lacks assurance that ISR capabilities approved through the JCIDS process provide joint solutions to DOD's ISR capability needs and are the solutions that best minimize inefficiency and redundancy. The BA FCB did not fully implement oversight activities for three key reasons. First, the BA FCB does not have a readily available source of information that identifies the full range of existing and developmental ISR capabilities, which would serve as a tool for reviewing the jointness and efficiency of the sponsors' assessments. Second, the BA FCB lacks a monitoring mechanism to ensure that key oversight activities are fully implemented as described in existing guidance. Third, BA FCB officials said that the BA FCB does not have adequate numbers of dedicated, skilled personnel to engage in early coordination with sponsors and review the sponsors' capabilities-based assessments. Since the BA FCB did not fully implement its oversight activities, neither the BA FCB nor the sponsors can be assured that the sponsors considered the full range of potential solutions when conducting their assessments and identified a joint approach to addressing warfighters' needs. To enable effective Joint Staff oversight over ISR capability development, we are recommending that the Secretary of Defense direct the Chairman of the Joint Chiefs of Staff and the USD(I) to collaborate in developing a comprehensive source of information on all ISR capabilities for use in informing capabilities-based assessments. We are also recommending that the Secretary of Defense direct the Chairman of the Joint Chiefs of Staff to develop a supervisory review or other monitoring mechanism to ensure that (1) the BA FCB and sponsors engage in early coordination to facilitate sponsors' consideration of existing and developmental ISR capabilities in developing their capabilities-based assessments, (2) capabilities-based assessments are completed, and (3) the BA FCB uses systematic procedures for reviewing the assessments. We are also recommending that the Secretary of Defense direct the Chairman of the Joint Chiefs of Staff to review the BA FCB's staffing levels and expertise and workload to engage in early coordination with sponsors and review their assessments, and, if shortfalls of personnel, resources, or training are identified, develop a plan for addressing them.

In written comments on a draft of this report, DOD agreed or partially agreed with our recommendations to develop a vision of a future ISR architecture, to develop a comprehensive source of information on all ISR capabilities, and to ensure that key activities—such as early coordination between the BA FCB and sponsors, and completion and review of assessments—are fully implemented. However, DOD stated that changes in guidance were not needed. DOD disagreed with our recommendation that it review the BA FCB's staffing levels and expertise and workload to engage in early coordination with sponsors and review their assessments, and, if shortfalls of personnel, resources, or training are identified, develop a plan for addressing them. In its comments, DOD noted that it had conducted a review of Functional Capabilities Board personnel and resources in fiscal year 2007 which did not identify deficiencies. However, workload issues and lack of technical skills among staff were mentioned to us by defense officials as reasons why early coordination and reviews of capabilities-based assessments were not being systematically performed as part of the BA FCB's oversight function. Therefore, in light of our finding that the BA FCB did not fully implement these key oversight activities as called for in Joint Staff policy, we believe that the department should reconsider whether the BA FCB has the appropriate number of staff with the appropriate skills to fully implement these oversight activities. In addition, based on DOD's comments, we modified one of our recommendations to clarify that the Secretary of Defense could assign leadership to either the Joint Staff or the USD(I), in consultation with the other, to develop the comprehensive source of information that the sponsors and the BA FCB need. In making this modification, we also moved two actions that were originally part of this recommendation and included them in another, thereby consolidating actions that the Joint Staff needs to take into one recommendation. Also in response to DOD's comments, we modified our recommendation related to ensuring that early coordination and completion and review of sponsors' assessments are conducted by clarifying that a monitoring mechanism is needed to ensure that DOD fully implement these key activities in accordance with existing guidance. DOD's comments are reprinted in appendix II.

Background

In 2001, DOD shifted from a threat-based planning process focused on preparing the department for a set of threat scenarios to a capabilities-based process focused on identifying what capabilities DOD would need to counter expected adversaries. The expectation was that a capabilities-based process would prevent DOD from over-optimizing for a limited set of scenarios. The 2006 Quadrennial Defense Review continued this shift in order to emphasize the needs of the combatant commanders by implementing portfolio management principles for cross-sections of DOD's capabilities. Portfolio management principles are commonly used by large commercial companies to prioritize needs and allocate resources. In September 2006, DOD initiated a test case of the portfolio management concept, which included DOD's management of its ISR capabilities. The USD(I) is the lead office for this ISR portfolio, and the ISR Integration Council, a group of senior DOD intelligence officers created as a forum for the services to discuss ISR integration efforts, acts as the governance body for the ISR portfolio management effort. In February 2008, DOD announced its plans to formalize the test cases, including the ISR portfolio, as standing capability portfolio management efforts.

DOD established JCIDS as part of its capabilities-based planning process and to be a replacement for DOD's previous requirements identification process, which, according to DOD, frequently resulted in systems that were service-focused rather than joint, programs that duplicated each other, and systems that were not interoperable. Under this previous process, requirements were often developed by the services as stand-alone solutions to counter specific threats and scenarios. In contrast, the JCIDS process is designed to identify the broad set of capabilities that may be required to address the security environment of the twenty-first century. In addition, requirements under the JCIDS process are intended to be developed from the "top-down," that is, starting with the national military strategy, whereas the former process was "bottom-up," with requirements growing out of the individual services' unique strategic visions and lacking clear linkages to the national military strategy.

The BA FCB has responsibilities that include both JCIDS and non-JCIDS activities. The BA FCB provides input on the ISR capability portfolio management test case to the USD(I), who leads the test case and who, in turn, often provides inputs to the BA FCB deliberations on ISR capability needs. The BA FCB also generally provides analytic support for Joint Staff discussions and decisions on joint concepts and programmatic issues. In addition, the BA FCB has responsibilities for helping to oversee materiel and non-materiel capabilities development within JCIDS.[12] To do this, the BA FCB reviews proposals for new ISR capabilities, as well as proposals for non-materiel ISR capabilities and for ISR capabilities already in development, and submits recommendations to the Joint Requirements Oversight Council on whether or not to approve them.[13] To support their proposals for new ISR capabilities, the sponsors are expected to conduct a robust, three-part capabilities-based assessment that identifies (1) warfighter skills and attributes for a desired capability (Functional Area Analysis), (2) the gaps to achieving this capability based on an assessment

---

[12] Joint Staff policy defines materiel capability solutions as resulting in the development, acquisition, procurement, or fielding of a new item, and defines non-materiel capability solutions as changes in doctrine, organization, training, materiel, leadership and education, personnel, facilities, or policy to satisfy identified functional capabilities. Chairman of the Joint Chiefs of Staff Instruction 3170.01F, *Joint Capabilities Integration and Development System* (May 1, 2007).

[13] For the purposes of this report, we use "proposals for non-materiel capabilities" to refer to Doctrine, Organization, Training, Materiel, Leadership and Education, Personnel, and Facilities Change Requests, and "proposals for capabilities already in development" to refer to Capability Development Documents and Capability Production Documents.

of all existing systems (Functional Needs Analysis), and (3) possible solutions for filling these gaps (Functional Solution Analysis). According to Joint Staff guidance, the latter assessment should consider the development of new systems, non-materiel solutions that do not require the development of new systems, modifications to existing systems, or a combination of these, as possible solutions to filling identified capability gaps. Figure 1 provides an overview of the JCIDS analysis process as it relates to proposals for new capabilities, showing that these proposals are supposed to flow from top-level defense guidance, including DOD strategic guidance, Joint Operations Concepts, and Concepts of Operations.[14] This guidance is to provide the conceptual basis for the sponsor's capabilities-based assessment, which ultimately results in the sponsor's proposal for a new capability.

---

[14] Joint Operations Concepts present a visualization of future operations, describing how future operations may be conducted and providing the conceptual basis for joint experimentation and capabilities-based assessments. A Concept of Operations is a statement of a commander's assumptions or intent in regard to an operation or series of operations, and is frequently embodied in campaign plans and operation plans. Chairman of the Joint Chiefs of Staff Instruction 3170.01F, *Joint Capabilities Integration and Development System* (May 1, 2007).

Figure 1: The JCIDS Analysis Process for Proposals for New Capabilities

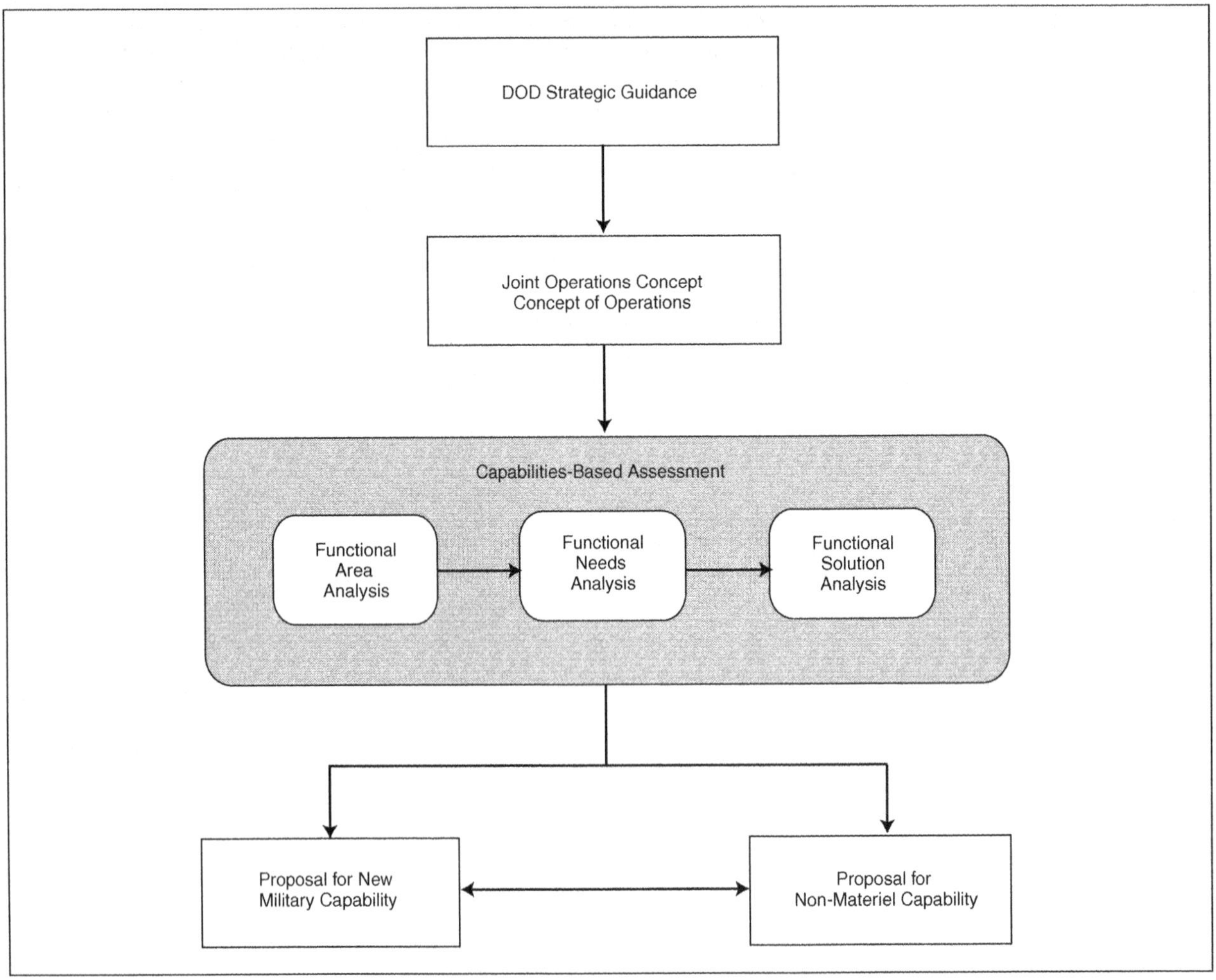

```
                    ┌──────────────────────────┐
                    │   DOD Strategic Guidance  │
                    └──────────────────────────┘
                                 │
                                 ▼
                    ┌──────────────────────────┐
                    │  Joint Operations Concept │
                    │   Concept of Operations   │
                    └──────────────────────────┘
                                 │
                                 ▼
         Capabilities-Based Assessment
     ┌──────────┐     ┌──────────┐     ┌──────────┐
     │Functional│ ──▶ │Functional│ ──▶ │Functional│
     │   Area   │     │  Needs   │     │ Solution │
     │ Analysis │     │ Analysis │     │ Analysis │
     └──────────┘     └──────────┘     └──────────┘
                                 │
                ┌────────────────┴────────────────┐
                ▼                                  ▼
     ┌────────────────────┐          ┌────────────────────┐
     │   Proposal for New │ ◀──────▶ │   Proposal for     │
     │ Military Capability│          │Non-Materiel Capability│
     └────────────────────┘          └────────────────────┘
```

Source: Joint Staff guidance.

The Wide Range of DOD ISR Enterprise Commitments across the U.S. Intelligence Community Presents a Challenging Environment for Greater DOD ISR Integration

DOD provides ISR capabilities in support of a wide range of defense and non-defense agencies across the intelligence community, creating a complex environment for DOD as it tries to integrate defense and national ISR capabilities. As DOD works to define its ISR capability requirements and improve integration of enterprisewide ISR capabilities, the department is faced with different and sometimes competing organizational cultures, funding arrangements, and requirements processes, reflecting the diverse missions of the many intelligence community agencies that DOD supports. This wide range of DOD ISR enterprise commitments across the U.S. intelligence community presents challenges for DOD as it works to increase ISR effectiveness and avoid unnecessary investments in ISR capabilities.

DOD's ISR Enterprise Supports a Wide Array of Intelligence Organizations, Making Greater Integration Complex

DOD's ISR enterprise is comprised of many organizations and offices from both the defense intelligence community and the national intelligence community. DOD relies on both its own ISR assets and national ISR assets to provide comprehensive intelligence in support of its joint warfighting force. For example, the National Reconnaissance Office, a DOD agency, provides overhead reconnaissance satellites which may be used by national intelligence community members such as the Central Intelligence Agency. Figure 2 demonstrates that DOD's ISR enterprise supports a wide range of intelligence community organizations.

Figure 2: DOD ISR Enterprise Relationship to the U.S. Intelligence Community

Director of National Intelligence

Under Secretary of Defense for Intelligence
designated as
Director of Defense Intelligence in the Office of the Director of National Intelligence

Defense Intelligence Community

Members:

- Defense Intelligence Agency
- National Security Agency
- National Reconnaissance Office
- National Geospatial-Intelligence Agency
- Military Service Intelligence Branches
  (Army, Navy, Air Force, Marine Corps)

National Intelligence Community

Members:

- Central Intelligence Agency
- Department of Homeland Security
- Department of Energy
- Department of the Treasury
- Department of State
- Federal Bureau of Investigation
- Drug Enforcement Agency
- Coast Guard

DOD ISR Enterprise

*Provides capabilities in support of missions across
the defense and national intelligence communities*

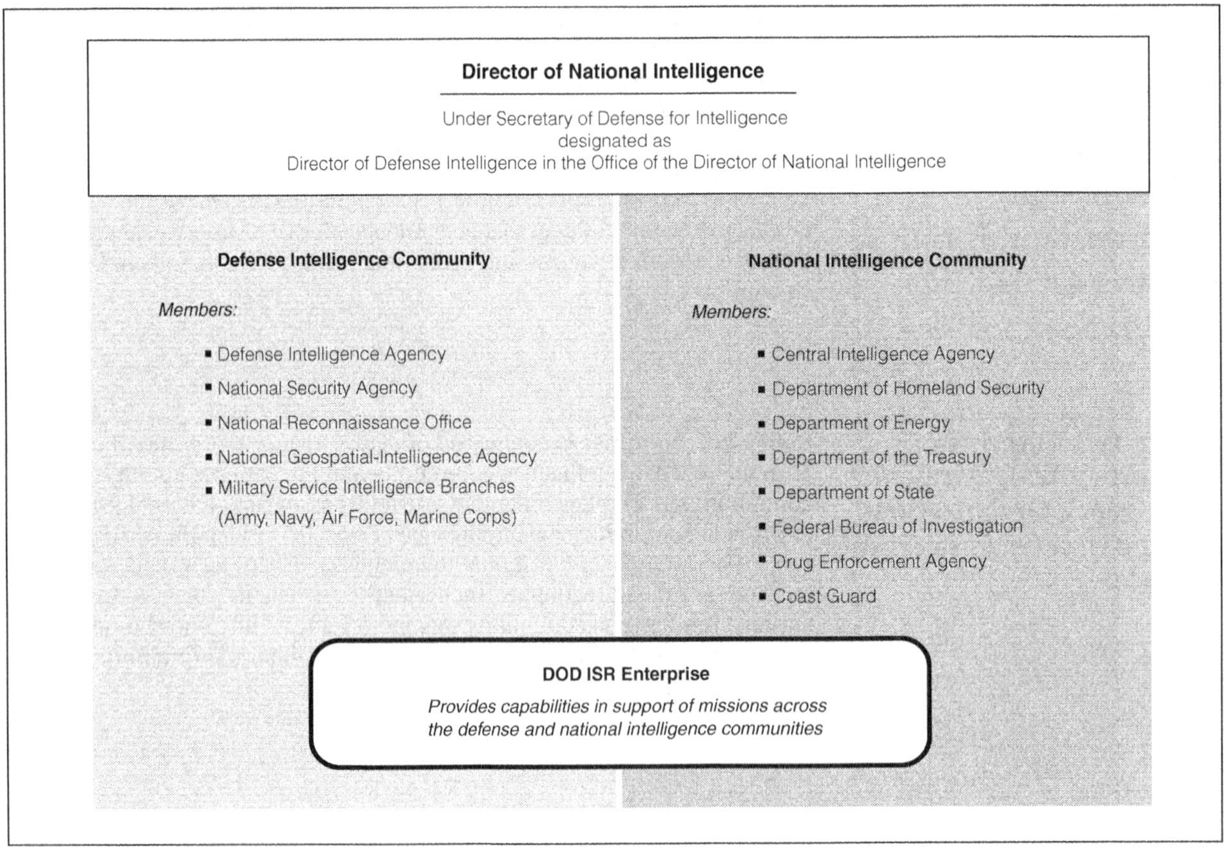

Source: GAO analysis.

DOD organizations are involved in providing intelligence information to both the defense and national intelligence communities, using their respective or joint ISR assets. In addition to the intelligence branches of the military services, there are four major intelligence agencies within DOD: the Defense Intelligence Agency; the National Security Agency; the National Geospatial-Intelligence Agency; and the National Reconnaissance Office. The Defense Intelligence Agency is charged with providing all-source intelligence data to policy makers and U.S. armed forces around the world. The Director of the Defense Intelligence Agency, a three-star military officer, serves as the principal intelligence advisor to the

GAO-08-374 Intelligence, Surveillance, and Reconnaissance

Secretary of Defense and the Chairman of the Joint Chiefs of Staff. The National Security Agency is responsible for signals intelligence and has collection sites throughout the world. The National Geospatial-Intelligence Agency prepares the geospatial data, including maps and computerized databases necessary for targeting in an era dependent upon precision-guided weapons. The National Reconnaissance Office develops and operates reconnaissance satellites. Although these are DOD intelligence agencies, all of these organizations nevertheless provide intelligence information to meet the needs of the national intelligence community as well as DOD. The National Reconnaissance Office, in particular, is a joint organization where ultimate management and operational responsibility resides with the Secretary of Defense in concert with the Director of National Intelligence. In addition, the national intelligence community includes agencies such as the Central Intelligence Agency, whose responsibilities include providing foreign intelligence on national security issues to senior policymakers, as well as the intelligence-related components of other federal agencies, all of which have different missions and priorities. For example, the intelligence component of the Department of State is concerned with using intelligence information, among other things, to support U.S. diplomatic efforts, while the intelligence component of the Department of Energy may use intelligence to gauge the threat of nuclear terrorism and counter the spread of nuclear technologies and material.

Different Organizational Cultures, Funding Arrangements, and Requirements Processes Present a Challenging Environment in Which to Coordinate DOD and National Intelligence Activities

The complex context of different organizational cultures, funding arrangements, requirements processes, and diverse missions of other members of the intelligence community that DOD supports presents a challenge for DOD in integrating its ISR enterprise, as highlighted by previous efforts to achieve greater ISR integration within DOD. Observers have noted in the past that cultural differences between the defense and national intelligence agencies and their different organizational constructs often impede close coordination. For example, Congress found in the past that DOD and the national intelligence community may not be well-positioned to coordinate their intelligence activities and programs, including ISR investments, in order to ensure unity of effort and avoid duplication of effort, and a congressionally chartered commission that reviewed the management and organization of national security space activities—known as the Space Commission—noted that understanding the different organizational cultures of the defense and national space communities is important for achieving long-term integration. Subsequently, in 2003 and 2004, a joint task force of the Defense Science Board observed that there was no procedural mechanism for resolving differences between DOD and the national intelligence community over requirements and funding for national security space programs.[15] In 2005, a private sector organization indicated that DOD and the intelligence community should improve their efforts to enhance information sharing and collaboration among the national security agencies of the U.S. government.[16] In addition, according to the ODNI, the traditional distinction between the intelligence missions of DOD and the national intelligence community have become increasingly blurred since the events of September 11, 2001, with DOD engaging in more strategic missions and the national intelligence community engaging in more tactical missions. Because of this trend, government decision makers have recognized the increased importance of ensuring effective coordination and integration between DOD and the national intelligence community in order to successfully address today's security threats. Two areas within DOD's ISR enterprise where coordination between DOD and the national intelligence community are important are: (1) managing funding and budget decisions for ISR capabilities, and (2) developing requirements for new ISR capabilities. DOD has two decision-support processes in place to conduct these functions: its Planning, Programming, Budgeting, and Execution process, and its Joint Capabilities Integration and Development System. However, DOD also coordinates with the Office of the Director of National Intelligence, which uses separate budgeting and requirements identification processes to manage the national intelligence budget.

Previous Efforts toward ISR Integration Highlight Organizational Challenges

Past DOD efforts to integrate its own ISR activities with those of the national intelligence community have shown the difficulty of implementing organizational changes that may appear counter to institutional culture and prerogatives. For example, in its January 2001 report, the Space Commission made recommendations to DOD to improve coordination, execution, and oversight of the department's space activities.[17] Among other things, the Space Commission stated that the

---

[15] Office of the Under Secretary of Defense for Acquisition, Technology, and Logistics, *Report of the Defense Science Board/Air Force Scientific Advisory Board Joint Task Force on Acquisition of National Security Space Programs* (Washington, D.C.: May 2003); Task Force on Acquisition of National Security Space Programs, *Summary of Findings: One Year Review* (July 27, 2004).

[16] Center for Strategic and International Studies, *Beyond Goldwater-Nichols: U.S. Government and Defense Reform for a New Strategic Era, Phase 2 Report* (Washington, D.C.: July 2005).

[17] Department of Defense, *Report of the Commission to Assess United States National Security Space Management and Organization* (Washington, D.C.: Jan. 11, 2001).

heads of the defense and national space communities should work closely and effectively together to set and maintain the course for national security space programs—a subset of ISR capabilities—and to resolve differences that arise between their respective bureaucracies. To accomplish this, the Space Commission called for the designation of a senior-level advocate for the defense and national space communities, with the aim of coordinating defense and intelligence space requirements. In response to this recommendation, in 2003 the department assigned to the DOD Executive Agent for Space the role of the Director of the National Reconnaissance Office, and the National Security Space Office was established to serve as the action agency of the DOD Executive Agent for Space. The National Security Space Office received both DOD and National Reconnaissance Office funding and was staffed by both DOD and National Reconnaissance Office personnel. However, in July 2005, the Secretary of Defense split the positions of the National Reconnaissance Office Director and the Executive Agent for Space by appointing an official to once again serve exclusively as the Director of the National Reconnaissance Office, citing the need for dedicated leadership at that agency. The National Reconnaissance Office Director subsequently removed National Reconnaissance Office personnel and funding from the National Security Space Office, and restricted the National Security Space Office's access to a classified information-sharing network, thereby inhibiting efforts to further integrate defense and national space activities—including ISR activities—as recommended by the Space Commission. In another case, DOD officials stated that, when developing the ISR Integration Roadmap, they had difficulty gaining information to include in the Roadmap on national-level ISR capabilities that were funded by the national intelligence budget.

Funding of ISR Assets across DOD and National Intelligence Budgets Presents a Challenge for ISR Integration Efforts

Spending on most ISR programs is divided between the national intelligence budget, known as the National Intelligence Program (NIP), and the defense intelligence budget, known as the Military Intelligence Program (MIP).

- The NIP consists of intelligence programs that support national decision makers, especially the President, the National Security Council, and the heads of cabinet departments, to include the Department of Defense. The Director of National Intelligence is responsible for developing and determining the annual NIP budget, which, according to the Office of the Director of National Intelligence, amounted to $43.5 billion appropriated for fiscal year 2007.[18] To assist in this task, officials from the Office of the Director of National Intelligence stated that they currently use a framework known as the Intelligence Community Architecture, the focus of which is to facilitate the Office of the Director of National Intelligence's intelligence budget deliberations by providing a set of repeatable processes and tools for decision makers to make informed investment decisions about what intelligence systems, including ISR systems, to buy. According to officials from the Office of the Director of National Intelligence, they are working with DOD to finalize guidance related to the Intelligence Community Architecture as of January 2008.

- The MIP encompasses DOD-wide intelligence programs and most intelligence programs supporting the operating units of the military services. The USD(I) is responsible for compiling and developing the MIP budget. To assist in informing its investment decisions for MIP-funded activities, the USD(I) is currently employing an investment approach that is intended to develop and manage ISR capabilities across the entire department, rather than by military service or individual program, in order to enable interoperability of future ISR capabilities and reduce redundancies and gaps. The total amount of the annual MIP budget is classified.

Given that DOD provides ISR capabilities to the national intelligence community, some defense organizations within DOD's ISR enterprise are funded through the NIP as well as the MIP. For example, three DOD intelligence agencies—the National Security Agency, the National Reconnaissance Office, and the National Geospatial-Intelligence Agency—are included in the NIP. While the Director of National Intelligence is responsible for preparing a NIP budget that incorporates input from NIP-funded defense agencies, such as the National Security Agency, National Reconnaissance Office, and National Geospatial-Intelligence Agency, USD(I) has responsibility for overseeing defense ISR capabilities within the NIP as well as within the MIP. The statutorily required guidelines to ensure the effective implementation of the Director of National Intelligence's authorities, including budgetary authority over defense intelligence agencies, had not been established as of January 2008.[19] In

---

[18] Section 601(a) of Pub. L. No. 110-53 requires the Director of National Intelligence to disclose to the public after the end of each fiscal year the aggregate amount of funds appropriated by Congress for the NIP for such fiscal year. In October 2007, the Director of National Intelligence disclosed the amount appropriated to the NIP for fiscal year 2007.

[19] Intelligence Reform and Terrorism Prevention Act of 2004, Pub. L. No. 108-458, § 1018.

recognition of the importance of coordinated intelligence efforts, the Secretary of Defense and the Director of National Intelligence signed a memorandum of agreement in May 2007 that assigned the USD(I) the role of Director of Defense Intelligence within the Office of the Director of National Intelligence, reinforcing the USD(I)'s responsibility for ensuring that the investments of both the defense and national intelligence communities are mutually supportive of each other's roles and missions. The specific responsibilities of this position were defined by a January 2008 agreement signed by the Director of National Intelligence, after consultation with the Secretary of Defense, but it is too early to know whether this new position will increase coordination between the defense and national intelligence communities with regard to planning for current and future spending on ISR capabilities.

Although DOD and the Office of the Director of National Intelligence have begun working together to coordinate funding mechanisms for joint programs, DOD efforts to ensure funding for major ISR programs that also support national intelligence missions can be complicated when funding for those systems is shared between the separate MIP and NIP budgets. For example, as the program executive for the DOD intelligence budget, the USD(I) is charged with coordinating DOD's ISR investments with those of the non-DOD intelligence community. A DOD official stated that, as part of the fiscal year 2008 ISR budget deliberations, the USD(I) and the Air Force argued that funding for the Space Based Infrared Radar System and Space Radar satellite systems, which are managed jointly by the Air Force and National Reconnaissance Office, should be shared between the DOD ISR budget and the national intelligence community ISR budget to better reflect that these programs support both DOD and national intelligence priorities. As a result, according to a DOD official, USD(I) negotiated a cost-sharing arrangement with the Director of National Intelligence, and, although the Air Force believed that its funding contribution under the cost-sharing agreement was too high, the Deputy Secretary of Defense ultimately decided that the Air Force would assume the higher funding level. A DOD official stated that the delay in funding for the Space Radar system caused its initial operational capability date to be pushed back by approximately one year.

Separate Defense and Non-Defense ISR Requirements Processes Add to Complexity of ISR Integration

In addition to having separate intelligence budgets, DOD and the Office of the Director of National Intelligence also conduct separate processes to identify future requirements.

- In DOD, proposals for new ISR capabilities are often developed by the individual services, which identify their respective military needs in accordance with their Title 10 responsibilities to train and equip their forces.[20] Proposals for new ISR capabilities may also be developed by defense agencies or combatant commands. Proposals for new ISR capabilities that support defense intelligence requirements may be submitted through DOD's JCIDS process, at which time the department is to review the proposals to ensure that they meet the full range of challenges that the services may face when operating together as a joint force.

- The Office of the Director of National Intelligence has its own separate process, carried out by the Mission Requirements Board, which is intended to serve as the approval mechanism for future national intelligence requirements as well as to provide input on future intelligence capabilities being acquired by DOD that may also support national intelligence community missions. According to officials from both the Office of the Director of National Intelligence and DOD, the process carried out by the Office of the Director of National Intelligence is evolving and is less formalized than DOD's JCIDS process.

These separate ISR requirements identification processes for DOD and the Office of the Director of National Intelligence may present challenges for DOD since there are not yet any standard procedures for ensuring that ISR capability proposals affecting both the defense and national intelligence communities are reviewed in a timely manner by both processes. Although there is coordination between the two processes, DOD officials related that the nature of the relationship between JCIDS and the Mission Requirements Board process is still unclear. Officials from the Office of the Director of National Intelligence confirmed that the structure of their office is still evolving, and therefore no standard process currently exists for determining what DOD capability proposals the Mission Requirements Board will review, or what criteria will be used to conduct such reviews. Officials from the Office of the Director of National Intelligence stated that Mission Requirements Board members exercise their professional judgment on which DOD systems need to be reviewed and whether enough of the capability is already being delivered by existing systems. Although there is a 2001 Director of Central Intelligence directive that establishes the Mission Requirements Board and calls upon it to oversee,

---

[20] Title 10 of the United States Code authorizes the secretaries of the military departments to conduct functions related to their personnel, including recruiting, organizing, training, and maintaining. 10 U.S.C. §§ 3013, 5013, 8013 (2007).

in consultation with DOD's Joint Requirements Oversight Council, the development of requirements documents that are common to both national and joint military operational users, this directive contains no specific criteria for doing so. Officials from the Office of the Director of National Intelligence stated that they are planning to update this 2001 directive on the Mission Requirements Board. Moreover, coordinating the separate requirements processes to ensure that an ISR capability proposal receives timely input on requirements from both DOD and the national intelligence community can be challenging. DOD and the Office of the Director of National Intelligence have not determined systematic procedures or clear guidance for handling situations in which they have different opinions on ISR capability proposals. For example, the Mission Requirements Board did not approve a proposal for a new ISR capability to ensure that the proposal incorporated certain changes, even though DOD had already given its approval to the proposal through the JCIDS process. The unclear nature of the relationship between DOD's and the Office of the Director of National Intelligence's ISR requirements identification processes may complicate DOD efforts to develop future ISR systems that provide capabilities across the defense and national intelligence communities.

DOD Has Initiatives to Improve the Integration of Its Future ISR Investments, but the Initiatives Do Not Provide Key Management Tools Needed to Effectively Guide ISR Investments

To improve the integration of its ISR investments, DOD has developed two initiatives—the ISR Integration Roadmap and a test case for managing ISR investments as part of a departmentwide portfolio of capabilities. [21] These initiatives are positive steps toward managing ISR investments from an enterprise-level perspective rather than from a service or agency perspective. However, our review has shown that these initiatives do not provide ISR decision makers with two key management tools: (1) a clearly defined vision of a future ISR enterprise that lays out what investments are needed to achieve strategic goals, and (2) a unified investment management approach with a framework that ISR decision makers can use to weigh the relative costs, benefits, and risks of proposed investments using established criteria and methods. Without these key tools, ISR decision makers lack a robust ISR analytical framework they can use to assess different ISR investments in order to identify the best return on investment in light of strategic goals. As a result, senior DOD leaders are not well-positioned to exert discipline over ISR spending to ensure ISR investments reflect enterprisewide priorities and strategic goals.

The ISR Roadmap Does Not Provide a Clear Vision of a Future ISR Enterprise That Lays Out What Capabilities Are Required to Achieve DOD's Strategic Goals

Based on our review and analysis, DOD's ISR Integration Roadmap does not yet provide (1) a clear vision of a future integrated ISR enterprise that identifies what ISR capabilities are needed to achieve DOD's strategic goals, or (2) a framework for evaluating tradeoffs between competing ISR capability needs and assessing how ISR capability investments contribute toward achieving those goals. DOD issued the ISR Integration Roadmap in May 2005 in response to a statutory requirement that directed USD(I) to develop a comprehensive plan to guide the development and integration of DOD ISR capabilities. DOD updated the Roadmap in January 2007. As we testified in April 2007, the Roadmap comprises a catalogue of detailed information on all the ISR assets being used and developed across DOD, including ISR capabilities related to collection, communication, exploitation, and analysis. Given the vast scope of ISR capabilities, which operate in a variety of media and encompass a range of intelligence disciplines, the ISR Integration Roadmap represents a significant effort on the part of DOD to bring together information needed to assess the strengths and weaknesses of current ISR capabilities. DOD officials have

---

[21] These two initiatives operate within the context of DOD's three decision-support processes: (1) the Joint Capabilities Integration and Development System, (2) the Defense Acquisition System, and (3) the Planning, Programming, Budgeting, and Execution system.

acknowledged that the Roadmap has limitations and stated that those limitations will be addressed in future revisions.

As DOD develops future revisions of the ISR Integration Roadmap, enterprise architecture is a valuable management tool that the department could use to develop a clear vision of a future ISR enterprise and a framework for evaluating tradeoffs between competing ISR needs and assessing how future ISR investments contribute to achieving strategic goals. Our previous work has shown that effective use of enterprise architecture is a hallmark of successful public and private organizations.[22] An enterprise architecture provides a clear and comprehensive picture of that organization, consisting of snapshots of its current (As-Is) state and its target (To-Be) state, and a transition plan for moving between the two states, and incorporates considerations such as technology opportunities, fiscal and budgetary constraints, legacy and new system dependencies and life expectancies, and the projected value of competing investments. DOD and federal guidance on enterprise architecture state that a framework for achieving an integrated enterprise should be based on a clearly defined target architecture, or vision, for a future enterprise derived from an analysis of the organization's future requirements and strategic goals.[23] A target architecture for the DOD ISR enterprise would (1) describe the structure of the future ISR enterprise and its desired capabilities in a way that is closely aligned with DOD ISR enterprise strategic goals, and (2) include metrics that facilitate evaluating tradeoffs between different investments and periodic assessment of progress toward achieving strategic goals. [24] Since it is likely that the architecture will evolve over time and be revised, it may also include an exploration of alternative investment options, and an acknowledgment of unknown factors. A clearly defined target architecture that depicts what ISR capabilities are required to achieve strategic goals would provide DOD with a framework for assessing its ISR capability gaps and overlaps by comparing its existing ISR capabilities to those laid out in the target architecture. Identified

---

[22] GAO, *DOD Business Systems Modernization: Important Progress Made in Establishing Foundational Architecture Products and Investment Management Practices, but Much Work Remains*, GAO-06-219 (Washington, D.C.: Nov. 23, 2005).

[23] Chief Information Officer Council, *A Practical Guide to Federal Enterprise Architecture, Version 1.0* (February 2001); Department of Defense, *Department of Defense Architecture Framework, Version 1.5* (April 2007).

[24] The term architecture refers to a description of the structure of an organization, the structure of its components, their interrelationships, and the principles and guidelines which govern their design and evolution over time.

capability gaps and overlaps would be the basis for guiding future ISR capability investments in order to transition the ISR enterprise from its current state toward the desired target architecture. Furthermore, as our previous work has emphasized, resources for investments such as those in ISR capabilities are likely to be constrained by fiscal challenges in the federal budget.[25] By clearly defining what ISR capabilities are required to achieve strategic goals over time, with metrics for assessing progress, an ISR target architecture would provide DOD with a framework for prioritizing its ISR investments when programs are affected by fiscal or technological constraints and an understanding of how changes to investment decisions in response to those constraints affect progress toward achieving strategic goals.

The ISR Integration Roadmap does not provide a clearly defined target architecture—or vision—of a future ISR enterprise or a framework for assessing progress toward achieving this vision because, in developing the Roadmap, USD(I) chose to take an incremental approach that limited it to articulating how capabilities already in DOD's existing ISR budget support strategic goals, rather than developing a longer term, more comprehensive target architecture based on an analysis of ISR capability needs beyond those defined in the existing DOD budget. In doing so, DOD did not fully address the time frame and subject areas listed in the statute. Congress tasked USD(I) to develop a plan to guide the development and integration of DOD ISR capabilities from 2004 through 2018, and to provide a report with information about six different management aspects of the ISR enterprise. However, USD(I) limited the Roadmap to the 5-year period covered by the existing ISR budget, and did not address three of the six areas the statute listed.[26] The three areas listed in the statute that USD(I) did not cover were (1) how DOD intelligence information could enhance DOD's role in homeland security, (2) how counterintelligence activities of

[25] GAO, *21st Century Challenges: Reexamining the Base of the Federal Government*, GAO-05-325SP (Washington, D.C.: February 2005).

[26] The 2004 National Defense Authorization Act (P.L. 108-136) amended Title 10 of the U.S. Code by adding section 426, which directed the Under Secretary of Defense for Intelligence to develop the ISR Integration Roadmap and to produce a report that addressed six management aspects of the ISR enterprise. DOD chose to provide information about these management aspects in the ISR Integration Roadmap. However, DOD covered only the first three of the six management areas specified in the statute: (1) the fundamental goals established in the Roadmap, (2) an overview of the ISR integration activities of the military departments and intelligence agencies of DOD, and (3) an investment strategy for achieving an integration of DOD ISR capabilities that ensures sustainment of needed tactical and operational efforts and efficient investment in new ISR capabilities.

the armed forces and DOD intelligence agencies could be better integrated, and (3) how funding authorizations and appropriations could be optimally structured to best support development of a fully integrated ISR architecture. USD(I) officials stated that due to the difficulty of projecting future operational requirements given ever-changing threats and missions, developing a detailed future ISR architecture beyond the scope of the capabilities already included in the 5-year ISR budget is very challenging. As such, the initial versions of the ISR Integration Roadmap were limited to the existing ISR budget.

Due to the limited scope of the ISR Integration Roadmap, it does not present a clear vision of what ISR capabilities are required to achieve strategic goals. In relying on DOD's existing ISR budget rather than developing a target architecture that details what ISR capabilities are required to achieve strategic goals, the Roadmap does not provide ISR decision makers with a point of reference against which to compare existing DOD ISR assets with those needed to achieve strategic goals. A clearly defined point of reference is needed to comprehensively identify capability gaps or overlaps. This limits the utility of the Roadmap as a basis of an ISR investment strategy linked to achieving strategic goals. For example, the most recent revision of the ISR Integration Roadmap lists global persistent surveillance as an ISR strategic goal but does not define the requirements for global persistent surveillance or how DOD will use current and future ISR assets to attain that goal. [27] The Roadmap states that the department will conduct a study to define DOD's complete requirements for achieving global persistent surveillance. The study was launched in 2006 but was limited to the planning and direction of ISR assets, which constitutes only one of the six intelligence activities, collectively known as the intelligence process, that would interact to achieve the global persistent surveillance goal.[28] Because the study is limited to only the planning and direction intelligence activity, it will not

---

[27] DOD defines persistent surveillance as the integrated management of a diverse set of collection and processing capabilities, operated to detect and understand the activity of interest with sufficient sensor dwell, revisit rate, and required quality to expeditiously assess adversary actions, predict adversary plans, deny sanctuary to an adversary, and assess results of U.S. or coalition actions.

[28] Planning and Direction is one of six activities collectively used to describe the intelligence process, which describes how the various types of interrelated intelligence activities interact to meet military commanders' needs. The other five areas are Collection, Processing and Exploitation, Analysis and Production, Dissemination and Integration, and Evaluation and Feedback.

examine whether there are capability gaps or overlaps in other areas, such as collection systems that include unmanned aircraft systems and satellites, or its intelligence information-sharing systems, and therefore is unlikely to define complete requirements for achieving this strategic goal. While DOD has other analytical efforts that could be used in assessing global persistent surveillance capability needs, these efforts are generally limited in scope to addressing the immediate needs of their respective sponsors. For example, U.S. Strategic Command's Joint Functional Component Command for ISR conducts assessments of ISR asset utilization and needs. However, these assessments are primarily intended to inform that organization's ISR asset allocation process, rather than to identify enterprisewide capability gaps with respect to strategic goals.

Further, lacking a target architecture, the Roadmap does not provide ISR decision makers a framework for evaluating tradeoffs between competing needs and assessing progress in achieving goals. As figure 3 illustrates, a clearly defined ISR target architecture would serve as a point of reference for ISR decision makers to develop a transition plan, or investment strategy for future ISR capability investments, based on an analysis that identifies capability gaps and overlaps against the ISR capabilities needed to achieve the target architecture, which would be based on DOD ISR strategic goals. Such an analysis would provide ISR decision makers with an underlying analytical framework to (1) quantify the extent of shortfalls, (2) evaluate tradeoffs between competing needs, and (3) derive a set of metrics to assess how future ISR investments contribute to addressing capability shortfalls. With this analytical framework, ISR decision makers at all levels of DOD would have a common set of analytical tools to understand how changing investment levels in different ISR capabilities would affect progress toward achieving goals. This same set of tools could be used by different ISR stakeholders evaluating how proposed ISR capabilities contribute to addressing different gaps or to possibly saturating a given capability area. For example, such a framework would allow ISR decision makers to identify areas where ISR collection capabilities are sufficiently robust or even saturated—areas where further investment may not be warranted given priority needs in other less robust collection areas.

Figure 3: Application of Enterprise Architecture Principles to the DOD ISR Enterprise

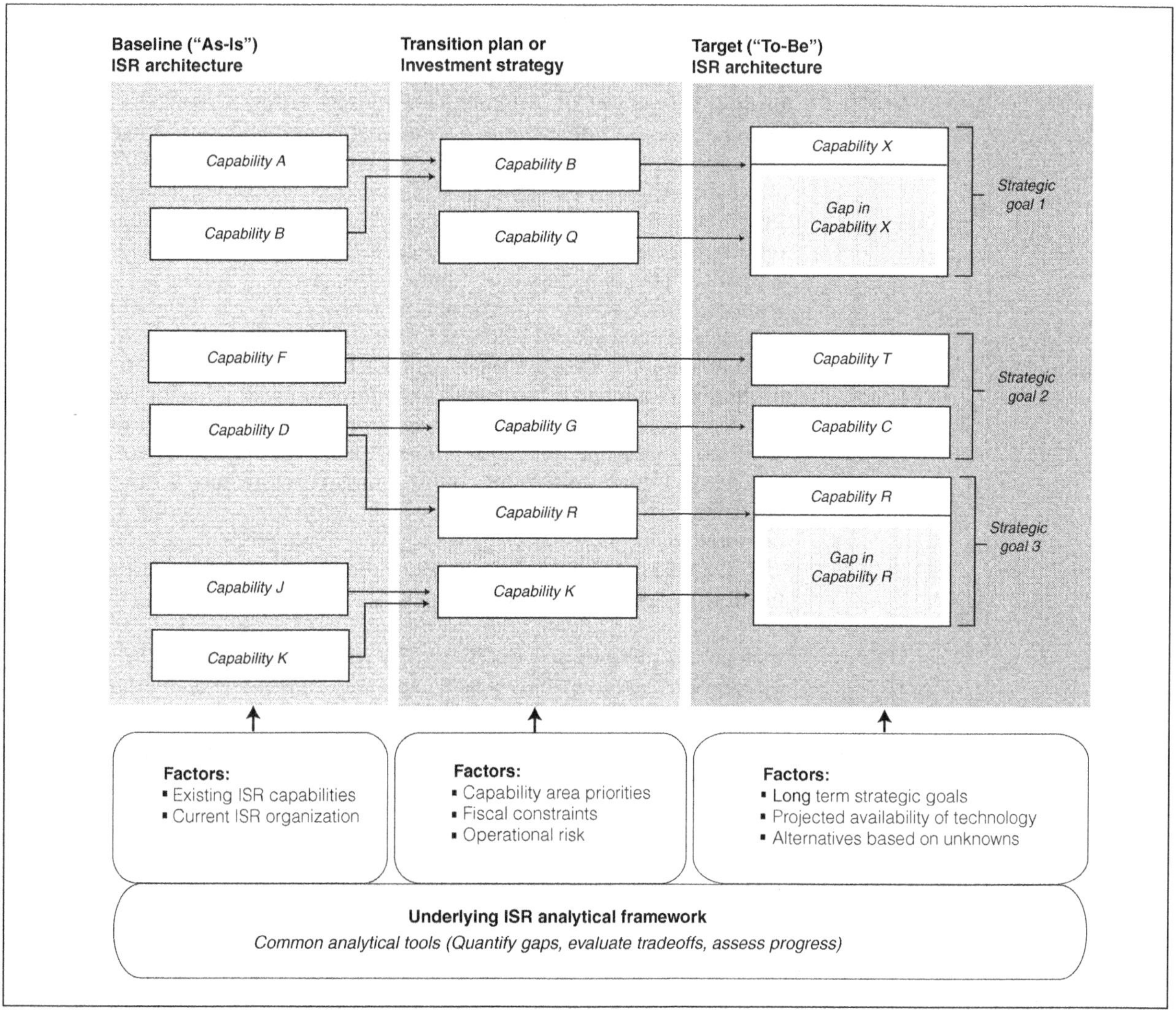

Baseline ("As-Is") ISR architecture

Transition plan or Investment strategy

Target ("To-Be") ISR architecture

| Capability A |
| Capability B |

| Capability B |
| Capability Q |

| Capability X |
| Gap in Capability X |

Strategic goal 1

| Capability F |

| Capability T |

Strategic goal 2

| Capability D |

| Capability G |

| Capability C |

| Capability R |

| Capability R |
| Gap in Capability R |

Strategic goal 3

| Capability J |
| Capability K |

| Capability K |

Factors:
- Existing ISR capabilities
- Current ISR organization

Factors:
- Capability area priorities
- Fiscal constraints
- Operational risk

Factors:
- Long term strategic goals
- Projected availability of technology
- Alternatives based on unknowns

Underlying ISR analytical framework
Common analytical tools (Quantify gaps, evaluate tradeoffs, assess progress)

Source: GAO analysis of federal enterprise architecure guidance.

Moreover, lacking a target architecture that depicts what capabilities are required to achieve DOD's strategic goals for the ISR enterprise, the Roadmap does not serve as a guide for the development of future ISR capabilities. A comprehensive source of information on how different ISR capabilities support strategic goals, and relate to other ISR capabilities, would be useful not only to ISR decision makers evaluating tradeoffs between competing needs, but also to program managers developing proposals for new ISR capabilities. Officials responsible for reviewing proposals for new ISR capabilities stated that a long-term vision of a future end state for the ISR enterprise would help sponsors to see what future ISR capabilities DOD needs and how their needs align with DOD's strategic goals. For example, officials from DOD's National Signatures Program said that, although they had a clear program goal in mind when developing their proposal for this new ISR capability, they experienced difficulty in developing an architecture because they lacked a comprehensive source of information to assess the full range of DOD and non-DOD databases and ISR assets that their proposed program would need to support.[29] Instead, these officials had to conduct an ad hoc survey of the ISR community, primarily in the form of meetings with other groups that maintained signatures databases, to ensure their program would be sufficiently interoperable with other information-sharing networks and ISR sensors. Without a clearly defined target architecture for the ISR enterprise, DOD lacks an analytical framework for conducting a comprehensive assessment of what investments are required to achieve ISR strategic goals, or for prioritizing investments in different areas when faced with competing needs.

Instead of providing an underlying analytical framework, the ISR Integration Roadmap simply lists capability gaps that exist with respect to DOD ISR strategic objectives, and depicts ISR capability investments already in the DOD ISR budget as fully meeting those capability shortfalls. For example, the Roadmap lists as an ISR strategic goal the achievement of "horizontal integration of intelligence information," which is broadly defined as making intelligence information within the defense intelligence enterprise more accessible, understandable, and retrievable. The Roadmap then lists a variety of ISR investments in DOD's 5-year ISR budget as the means of achieving this strategic goal. For example, one of these investments is the Distributed Common Ground System, a major DOD intelligence information-sharing network that spans the entire DOD intelligence community. However, the Roadmap does not present an

---

[29] The goal of the National Signatures Program is to develop a comprehensive enterprisewide database for cataloguing and sharing measurement and signals intelligence data, which uses the unique characteristics of physical objects, known as their signatures, to detect, track, and identify those objects.

analysis to facilitate evaluation of tradeoffs in that it does not quantify how the Distributed Common Ground System and other DOD information-sharing networks fall short of meeting the "horizontal integration of intelligence information" strategic goal, nor does it examine the extent to which some aspects of that capability area may in fact be saturated. Furthermore, the Roadmap does not prioritize investments in the Distributed Common Ground System with other major investments intended to achieve this strategic goal, or define their interrelationships. Finally, the Roadmap does not provide metrics to allow decision makers to assess how these investments contribute to achieving the "horizontal integration of intelligence information" strategic goal. For example, if the Distributed Common Ground System were to face fiscal or technological constraints, ISR decision makers would not have the information needed to assess what the impact would be on ISR strategic goals if it should not achieve those capability milestones as envisioned in the Roadmap. As a result, ISR decision makers cannot assess how new ISR capabilities would contribute to elimination of whatever capability gaps exist in that area, determine the most important gaps to fill, or make tough go/no-go decisions if those capabilities do not meet expectations.

The ISR Portfolio Management Effort Does Not Facilitate a Unified Investment Approach Needed to Guide DOD's ISR Investments

While DOD's ISR portfolio management effort is intended to enable the department to better integrate its ISR capabilities, it does not provide a framework for effectively evaluating different ISR investment options or clearly empower the ISR portfolio manager to direct ISR spending. As a result, DOD is not well-positioned to implement a unified investment approach that exerts discipline over ISR investments to ensure they reflect enterprisewide priorities and achieve strategic goals. In September 2006, the Deputy Secretary of Defense decided to bring ISR systems across the DOD together into a capability portfolio as part of a test case for the joint capability portfolio management concept. Under this concept, a group of military capabilities, such as ISR capabilities, is managed as a joint portfolio, in order to enable DOD to develop and manage ISR capabilities across the entire department—rather than by military service or individual program—and by doing so, to improve the interoperability of future capabilities, minimize capability redundancies and gaps, and maximize capability effectiveness. The USD(I) was assigned as the lead office for this ISR portfolio, which is known as the battlespace awareness portfolio.[30] As the portfolio manager for ISR investments, the role and authorities of the USD(I) are limited to two primarily advisory functions: (1) USD(I) is given access to, and may participate in, service and DOD agency budget deliberations on proposed ISR capability investments, and (2) USD(I) may recommend that service and DOD agency ISR spending be altered as part of the established DOD budget review process.[31] Under this arrangement, USD(I)'s recommendations represent one of many points of view that are considered by the Deputy Secretary of Defense and other DOD offices involved in reviewing and issuing budget guidance, and therefore USD(I) lacks the ability to ensure ISR spending reflects enterprisewide priorities to achieve strategic goals.

Our previous work on portfolio management best practices has shown that large organizations, such as DOD's ISR enterprise, are most successful in managing investments through a single enterprisewide approach.[32] Further, to be effective, portfolio management is enabled by strong governance with committed leadership, clearly aligned organizational roles and responsibilities, and portfolio managers empowered to determine the best way to invest resources. To achieve a balanced mix of programs and ensure a good return on their investments, successful large commercial companies that we have reviewed take a unified, enterprise-level approach to assessing new investments, rather than employing multiple, independent initiatives. They weigh the relative costs, benefits, and risks for proposed investments using established criteria and methods, and select those investments that can best move the company toward meeting its strategic goals and objectives. Their investment decisions are frequently revisited to ensure products are still of high value, and if a product falls short of expectations, they make tough go/no-go decisions.

---

[30] The other test cases are Joint Command and Control, Joint Net-Centric Operations, and Joint Logistics. In February 2008, DOD announced its plans to formalize these test cases, including the ISR portfolio, as standing capability portfolio management efforts, and to experiment with five additional portfolios, namely, Building Partnerships, Force Protection, Force Support, Force Application, and Corporate Management and Support.

[31] Based on the results of the budget and program review, final budget change decisions by the Secretary or Deputy Secretary of Defense are reflected in periodic guidance documents issued to instruct the military services or DOD agencies and direct them to make changes to their budgets.

[32] GAO, *Best Practices: An Integrated Portfolio Management Approach to Weapons System Investments Could Improve DOD's Acquisition Outcomes*, GAO-07-388 (Washington, D.C.: Mar. 30, 2007).

We have previously recommended that DOD establish portfolio managers who are empowered to prioritize needs, make early go/no-go decisions about alternative solutions, and allocate resources within fiscal constraints.[33] However, since DOD is still developing the capability portfolio management effort, it has not fully defined the role of the portfolio managers or their authority over spending. DOD's September 2006 guidance on the implementation of the portfolio management test case discusses options for increased authority over spending for the portfolio managers.[34] Nevertheless, USD(I) and DOD officials involved in the implementation of the portfolio management effort stated that DOD views the role of the portfolio managers primarily as providing an assessment of spending in their respective portfolio areas independent of the analysis offered by the military services in support of their ISR spending proposals. If USD(I)'s portfolio management role is limited to an advisory function as DOD moves forward in implementing its portfolio management effort, situations where senior DOD officials must evaluate the merits of alternate analyses that advocate different solutions to ISR capability needs are likely to continue to arise. A robust ISR analytical framework based on a well-defined ISR target architecture would establish a common methodology and criteria, as called for by portfolio management best practices, that is agreed upon by the various ISR stakeholders and that can be used for conducting a data-driven assessment of different ISR capability solutions. For example, as part of fiscal year 2008 ISR budget deliberations, USD(I) conducted an analysis of planned increases in fiscal year 2008 funding to procure more Predator unmanned aircraft systems in order to meet U.S. Central Command's need for increased surveillance capability.[35] U.S. Central Command and the Air Force conducted an analysis that was based on validating the requirement for more aircraft, rather than on examining potential efficiencies in other

---

[33] GAO-07-388.

[34] The Deputy Secretary of Defense defined the portfolio manager's role in a September 2006 memorandum. The memorandum outlines two different levels of increased authority over spending that portfolio managers may request to fulfill their responsibilities. A subsequent Deputy Secretary of Defense memorandum, issued in March 2007, discussed the portfolio manager's role in the fiscal year 2009 and 2010 budget deliberations, but did not enhance their authority over spending. In February 2008, the Deputy Secretary of Defense issued another memorandum, which stated that portfolio managers make recommendations on capability development issues within their portfolio but do not have independent decision-making authority.

[35] The Predator is a medium-altitude, long-endurance, remotely-piloted aircraft used primarily for conducting armed reconnaissance against critical targets.

aspects of employing them. As the ISR portfolio manager, USD(I)'s analysis focused on identifying opportunities for increased efficiencies in how existing Predators were being employed in surveillance missions. USD(I) determined, among other things, that Predator support to deployed forces was not being maximized because each ground control station could only operate one Predator aircraft at a time, resulting in gaps in the coverage of a target as Predator aircraft rotated to and from the launch area. On the basis of this analysis, USD(I) concluded that planned increases in fiscal year 2008 Predator spending may not be the best, or only, solution to U.S. Central Command's need for more surveillance capability; instead, the solution should include additional Predator ground control stations, or the tasking of other ISR assets in situations where a Predator would have longer transit times to and from the target area. The ISR Integration Council agreed with the USD(I)'s recommendation. Ultimately, the Deputy Secretary of Defense, who makes final decisions on changes advocated by the ISR portfolio manager, included the increase in Predator aircraft spending in the fiscal year 2008 budget. However, lacking a single, agreed-upon framework within the ISR enterprise for evaluating the merits of the alternate analyses advocating different capability solutions, DOD officials did not have the benefit of a single, authoritative analysis that identified the best return on investment of these different ISR investment options in light of strategic goals and validated requirements. Given USD(I)'s limited authority as the ISR capability portfolio manager, and the lack of a framework for effectively evaluating alternate investment plans, DOD is constrained in its ability to implement an enterprise-level, unified investment approach that employs a single set of established criteria to ensure its ISR investments reflect enterprisewide priorities and strategic goals.

DOD Has Not Fully Implemented Its Process to Develop, Integrate, and Approve Future ISR Capabilities

DOD has not implemented key activities within the JCIDS process to ensure that proposed new ISR capabilities are filling gaps, are not duplicative, and use a joint approach to addressing warfighters' needs. The services and DOD organizations that sponsored most of the JCIDS proposals for new ISR capabilities since 2003 have not conducted comprehensive assessments, and the BA FCB has not fully conducted key oversight activities. Specifically, our review of 19 proposals for new ISR capabilities that sponsors submitted to the BA FCB since 2003 showed that 12 sponsors did not complete the capabilities-based assessment of current and planned ISR systems called for by Joint Staff policy in order to identify possible solutions to meet warfighters' needs. We also found that, for the 7 sponsors who did conduct these assessments, the assessments varied in completeness and rigor. Moreover, we found that the BA FCB did not systematically coordinate with the sponsors during the sponsors' assessment process to help ensure the quality of the assessments, and did not generally review the assessments once they were completed. As a result, DOD lacks assurance that ISR capabilities approved through JCIDS provide joint solutions to DOD's ISR capability needs and are the solutions that best minimize inefficiency and redundancy.

Lack of Complete and Rigorous Analysis Hampers DOD's Process That Informs the Development of Its ISR Capabilities

Joint Staff policy and guidance implementing the JCIDS process, as well as a significant DOD study on defense capabilities,[36] indicate the importance of analyzing capability needs from a crosscutting, department-level perspective to enable a consistent view of priorities and acceptable risks. Specifically, Joint Staff policy[37] on the JCIDS process calls for sponsors to use a robust analytical process to ensure that the proposed ways to fill capability gaps are joint and efficient to the maximum extent possible.[38] This analytical process is known as a capabilities-based assessment, and Joint Staff policy and guidance specify that a capabilities-based assessment should include an analysis of the full range of existing and developmental ISR capabilities to confirm whether a shortcoming in mission performance exists, and of possible ways to fix those shortcomings, such as modifications to existing systems and the use of national-level systems. Nonetheless, Joint Staff guidance also notes that the breadth and depth of a capabilities-based assessment must be tailored to suit the issue, due to the wide array of issues considered as part of the capabilities-based assessment process.[39]

---

[36] The Joint Defense Capabilities Study Team, *Joint Defense Capabilities Study: Improving DOD Strategic Planning, Resourcing, and Execution to Satisfy Joint Capabilities, Final Report* (January 2004), alternatively known as the Aldridge Report.

[37] Chairman of the Joint Chiefs of Staff Instruction 3170.01F, *Joint Capabilities Integration and Development System* (May 1, 2007) and Chairman of the Joint Chiefs of Staff Instruction 3137.01C, *The Functional Capabilities Board Process* (Nov. 12, 2004).

[38] Ways to fill capability gaps are called solutions and may be either materiel or non-materiel.

[39] Chairman of the Joint Chiefs of Staff Manual 3170.01C, *Operation of the Joint Capabilities Integration and Development System* (May 1, 2007).

The Majority of ISR Capability Proposals Lacked Assessments Called for under the JCIDS Process

Despite Joint Staff policy that calls for capabilities-based assessments, we found that 12 sponsors—almost two-thirds—did not carry out capabilities-based assessments to identify the ISR capabilities that they proposed to the Joint Staff as ways to meet warfighters' needs. Figure 4 lists the 19 ISR capability proposals we reviewed and specifies which proposals were supported by capabilities-based assessments. [40] Figure 4 also shows that three of the proposals that lacked capabilities-based assessments were ones that DOD expected to cost more than $365 million for research, development, test and evaluation, or more than $2.190 billion for procurement, using fiscal year 2000 constant dollars. [41]

---

[40] Since implementing JCIDS in 2003, the Joint Staff updated its JCIDS policy and guidance three times, in 2004, 2005, and 2007. The most recent JCIDS guidance contains a list of questions to serve as procedural guidance for sponsors in conducting their capabilities-based assessments, although Joint Staff officials said it is not mandatory for sponsors to use this list. In addition, the Joint Staff issued separate guidance on conducting capabilities-based assessments in January 2006, updating it in December 2006. However, our review demonstrated that this guidance did not contribute greatly to the execution of more rigorous capabilities-based assessments.

[41] These are proposals that DOD designated as Acquisition Category I, the category assigned to DOD's highest cost programs. For more information about this and DOD's other acquisition programs, see DOD Instruction 5000.2, *Operation of the Defense Acquisition System* (May 12, 2003).

Figure 4: List of Proposals with and without Assessments, and Those with Highest Expected Cost Since 2003

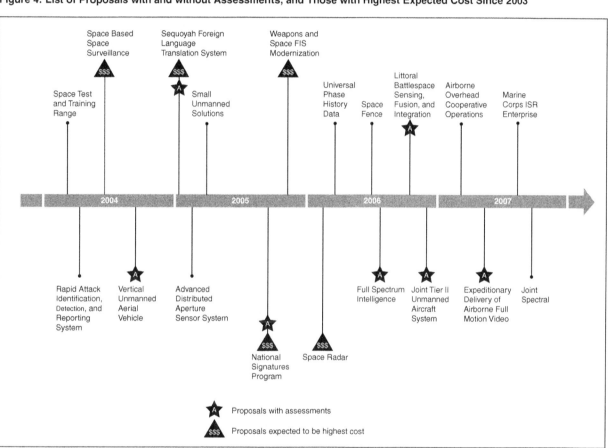

Source: GAO analysis of DOD documents.

Note: Line spacing indicating date of ISR capability proposals is sequential but not proportional. Also, the chronology reflects the date listed on each ISR capability proposal, which may not be the same as the date on which the proposal was reviewed by the BA FCB.

The 12 sponsors that did not conduct capabilities-based assessments, as called for under the JCIDS process, cited the following reasons for not doing them:

• Sponsors decided to use pre-existing analysis as an alternative to the capabilities-based assessment. Many of the sponsors that did not conduct formal capabilities-based assessments nevertheless based their proposals for new ISR capabilities on other forms of analysis or pre-existing mission needs statements. For example, Air Force sponsors stated that they supported their ISR capability proposal with analysis conducted in 1998 and 1999 and a mission needs statement from 2002, before JCIDS was implemented, while National Security Agency sponsors used the results of a substantial analytical effort they had completed just prior to the implementation of JCIDS in 2003. We did not evaluate these alternative types of analysis because they were not required to take the form of capabilities-based assessments as called for by Joint Staff policy and guidance on JCIDS.

- Sponsors had developed the capabilities prior to the implementation of JCIDS. Two Air Force proposals, both submitted to the Joint Staff in 2004, lacked capabilities-based assessments and, according to the sponsors of each, the Air Force had previously developed ISR systems that were similar to those described in their proposals prior to the implementation of JCIDS. Once JCIDS was implemented, the sponsor sought to obtain Joint Staff approval through the new process; since their ISR systems were already in development and pre-JCIDS analysis may have been conducted, the sponsors did not conduct the capabilities-based assessments. Other sponsors that had developed ISR systems prior to JCIDS being implemented nevertheless conducted capabilities-based assessments when they submitted their proposals. For example, one sponsor developed its proposal and performed its assessment at least 2 years after its organization officially established the program, and another sponsor's proposal was for a capability to be delivered through an upgrade of an aircraft developed in the late 1960s. These sponsors also sought approval for their ISR systems through the new JCIDS process, but since their systems were already in development, our review showed that these sponsors' capabilities-based assessments indicated they had the solution already in mind when conducting the assessments.

- Sponsors developed the capabilities through DOD processes other than JCIDS. Joint Staff policy allows for sponsors to develop a new capability through processes other than JCIDS and then later submit it to the Joint Staff for approval through JCIDS. For example, one sponsor said that it did not perform an assessment prior to developing its proposal because the service originally developed and validated the proposed capability through a technology demonstration process separate from the JCIDS process.[42]

- Sponsors lacked clear guidance on the JCIDS process, including how to conduct a capabilities-based assessment. One Air Force sponsor that submitted an ISR capability proposal in 2005 said that the Joint Staff policy implementing the JCIDS process was relatively new at the time, and did not contain clear guidance about how to conduct a capabilities-based assessment. Another sponsor did not conduct an assessment because the ISR capability it sought to develop was not a system, but rather a way of carrying out ISR-related activities, and it believed that, in such cases, a capabilities-based assessment was not expected.

- Sponsors had limited time and resources in which to carry out a capabilities-based assessment. Two sponsors cited lack of resources, including time, as a reason for not conducting a capabilities-based assessment. In one of these cases, the sponsor noted that conducting a capabilities-based assessment would not likely have resulted in a different type of capability being proposed to the Joint Staff.

One-Third of ISR Capability Proposals Included Assessments, but Assessments Varied in Rigor and Completeness

Our review found that 7 of the 19 sponsors conducted capabilities-based assessments, but these assessments varied in rigor and completeness. For example, 4 of these 7 sponsors did not include the cost information called for by Joint Staff guidance and 1 sponsor completed only one phase of the capabilities-based assessment. Figure 5 shows the 7 sponsors that did conduct capabilities-based assessments in support of their proposals and the extent to which these assessments contained elements called for by Joint Staff policy and guidance. We assessed these proposals as lacking an element called for by Joint Staff policy and guidance when our document review of the sponsor's capabilities-based assessment found no evidence of the element. Additional information about our methodology for conducting this analysis is contained in appendix I.

---

[42] DOD has an Advanced Concept Technology Demonstration program that is aimed at getting new technologies that meet critical military needs into the hands of users faster and for less cost.

Figure 5: Extent to Which Seven ISR Capability Proposals Since 2003 Included a Capabilities-Based Assessment That Incorporated Key Elements of Joint Staff Policy and Guidance[a]

Sponsoring organization	ISR capability proposal	Completeness of analytical support		Rigor of analytical support		
		Full review conducted	Cost information provided	Full range of existing and developmental ISR capabilities considered	Potential modifications considered	Potential redundancies considered
Air Force	Expeditionary Delivery of Airborne Full Motion Video	Partially	Yes	No	Partially	No
Army	Sequoyah Foreign Language Translation System	Partially	No	Partially	Partially	No
Defense Intelligence Agency	National Signatures Program	Partially	No	Partially	Partially	Yes
Marine Corps	Joint Tier II Unmanned Aircraft System	Yes	Partially	Partially	Partially	Partially
Marine Corps	Vertical Unmanned Aerial Vehicle	Yes	Yes	Partially	Partially	Partially
Navy	Full Spectrum Intelligence	Yes	Yes	Partially	Yes	No
Navy	Littoral Battlespace Sensing, Fusion, and Integration	Partially	No	Partially	Partially	No

● Yes
◖ Partially
○ No

Source: GAO analysis of DOD documents.

[a]Joint Staff policy and guidance with regard to figure 5 refers to Chairman of the Joint Chiefs of Staff Manuals 3170.01(2003), 3170.01A (2004), 3170.01B (2005), and 3170.01C (2007), and Chairman of the Joint Chiefs of Staff Instruction 3170.01F (2007).

The majority of the seven capabilities-based assessments that we reviewed did not consider the full range of existing ISR capabilities, including the use of national systems, such as satellites, as potential ways to fill identified shortcomings. For example, only one assessment documented that the sponsor had considered the use of national systems. Specifically, one Air Force sponsor's capabilities-based assessment showed consideration of the use of satellites to assist in quickly sending intelligence information gathered by unmanned aircraft systems to the warfighter in theater. The remaining six sponsors did not demonstrate in their capabilities-based assessments that they had fully assessed the use of national systems, although two of the assessments addressed capabilities that were unlikely to utilize national systems as potential solutions, such as a foreign language translation capability and an intelligence database. The sponsors who did not fully assess the potential for national systems to fill gaps gave a number of reasons for this. Navy sponsors of a manned platform told us that satellites were not included among the ways that they considered to fill capability gaps because the personnel conducting the assessment did not possess the appropriate security clearances needed to evaluate national systems and because of lack of time. Moreover, Marine Corps sponsors reported that neither of their two unmanned aircraft system capability proposals fully evaluated the use of satellites as potential ways to meet ISR needs because they assumed that satellites could not be quickly re-tasked to support the tactical user and lacked the imagery quality needed. In one of their assessments, they noted that satellite data, when available, are not responsive enough to the tactical user due to the long processing time, and that tactical users of satellite data also face challenges resulting from lack of connectivity between the systems that provide these data. In the other assessment, Marine Corps sponsors stated that one of their assumptions in conducting the analysis was that satellites, as well as theater-level unmanned aircraft systems, would not be available to support Marine Corps tactical operations.

All seven sponsors that conducted capabilities-based assessments considered the capacity of some existing and developing systems to meet capability gaps, but none documented in their assessments whether and how these systems could be modified to fill capability gaps—a potentially less expensive and less time-consuming solution than developing a new system. In some cases, DOD achieved efficiencies by combining related acquisition programs, although these actions were not the result of sponsors proactively seeking reduced overlap and duplication. For example, in the capabilities-based assessment for one of its two unmanned aircraft systems, Marine Corps sponsors identified several solutions with the potential to provide an ISR capability using existing or planned assets. Identified solutions included relying on or adopting systems provided by other services. In this case, the sponsors did not propose modifications to any existing systems as potential solutions or demonstrate that they considered leveraging the capabilities resident in a similar Navy unmanned aircraft system. The Joint Staff approved this proposal and Marine Corps officials plan to develop a new system that addresses Marine Corps warfighting requirements for vertical takeoff and landing capability for use on ships. In contrast, in another case involving a proposed capability sponsored by the Marine Corps, at the direction of the Assistant Secretary of the Navy for Research, Development, and Acquisition, the Marine Corps combined its unmanned aircraft system program with a different Navy effort to form a single acquisition program, with the goal of producing an integrated and interoperable solution, reducing costs, and eliminating overlap and duplication of development efforts. In this case, the JCIDS process did not help to identify the potential for collaboration on similar ISR capabilities.

The majority of sponsors' capabilities-based assessments that we reviewed did not mention redundancies that existed or might result from the development of their proposed new ISR capabilities. Specifically, only three of the seven sponsors demonstrated that they had considered potential redundancies in ISR capabilities when conducting their assessments. For example, the Defense Intelligence Agency sponsor of a proposal to develop a database cited the need to reduce redundant data systems as a reason for its proposed capability. In addition, a Marine Corps sponsor noted in its capabilities-based assessment that existing ISR systems are experiencing overlaps in five capability areas related to identification, monitoring, and tracking. Despite these examples of identified redundancies in existing ISR capabilities, all of the sponsors concluded that important capability gaps still existed and submitted proposals that supported the development of a new ISR capability.

The seven sponsors of the capabilities-based assessments that were not thorough and complete provided similar reasons as those provided by the sponsors that did not conduct capabilities-based assessments at all—for example, a shortage of time and resources and confusion about what was required under the JCIDS process. In addition, some sponsors had already developed a capability, or had the intended solution in mind, when conducting their capabilities-based assessments. Moreover, sponsors that conducted the assessments were hindered by a lack of comprehensive information on existing and developmental ISR capabilities that might potentially be used to fill the identified capability gap, and so could not use this information to fully inform their assessments. Several sponsors that conducted assessments told us that they faced challenges in identifying the full range of existing and developmental-stage ISR systems, in part because no centralized source of information existed. For example, Army sponsors of a language translation capability said that, despite use of personal connections and outreach to identify existing and developmental technologies, it was only after they had finished their capabilities-based assessment that they learned of a particular ISR technology that could have informed their assessment. Sponsors agreed that a source of readily available information on existing and developmental ISR capabilities would be useful.

DOD Has Not Fully Implemented Key Oversight Activities in the Process for Developing Future ISR Capabilities

Although the BA FCB's mission includes engaging in coordination during the sponsors' assessment process and providing oversight[43] of potential solutions to achieve optimum effectiveness and efficiency in ISR capability development, the BA FCB did not systematically coordinate with the sponsors to help ensure the quality of their capabilities-based assessments, nor did it routinely review those assessments once they were completed. The BA FCB did not implement these activities because it lacks a readily available source of information that identifies all ISR capabilities that would serve as a tool for reviewing the efficiency of sponsors' assessments, and because the BA FCB does not have a monitoring mechanism, which could ensure that key oversight activities are fully implemented, as described in Joint Staff policy. In addition, BA FCB officials said that they lack adequate numbers of dedicated, skilled personnel to engage in early coordination with the sponsors and review the sponsors' capabilities-based assessments. As a result, DOD cannot be assured that ISR capabilities approved through JCIDS provide joint solutions to DOD's ISR capability needs and are the solutions that best minimize inefficiency and redundancy.

DOD Did Not Ensure Quality of Sponsors' Assessments through Coordination with Sponsors or Review of Assessments

As described in Joint Staff policy, each Functional Capabilities Board's mission is to provide assessments and recommendations to enhance capabilities integration, examine joint priorities among existing and future programs, minimize duplication of effort throughout the services, and provide oversight of potential solutions to achieve optimum effectiveness and efficiency. Moreover, Joint Staff policy states that each Functional Capabilities Board's functions include assisting in overseeing capabilities development within JCIDS through assessment of proposals for new or improved capabilities.[44] The BA FCB is the Functional Capabilities Board that holds responsibility for the ISR functional area and, as such, is responsible for seeking to ensure that the joint force is best served throughout the JCIDS process.[45] Additionally, Joint Staff policy calls on

---

[43] We define oversight to include review of capabilities-based assessments, as well as coordination activities. Through these assessment and coordination activities, the BA FCB serves an internal control function, providing oversight to help ensure that DOD's objectives for its ISR enterprise are met through the JCIDS process.

[44] Chairman of the Joint Chiefs of Staff Instruction 3137.01C, *The Functional Capabilities Board Process* (Nov. 12, 2004) provides a complete list of Functional Capabilities Board functions.

[45] Chairman of the Joint Chiefs of Staff Instruction 3170.01F, *Joint Capabilities Integration and Development System* (May 1, 2007) also describes the responsibilities of the Functional Capabilities Boards.

each Functional Capabilities Board and its working group[46] to perform coordination functions within its respective capability area, to include (1) engaging in coordination throughout the sponsors' assessment process in order to promote cross-service efficiencies, and (2) coordinating and integrating departmentwide participation to ensure that sponsors' assessments adequately leverage the expertise of the DOD components to identify promising solutions. Through these assessment and coordination functions, as well as other feedback avenues, the BA FCB provides the analytical underpinnings in support of the Chairman of the Joint Chiefs of Staff's Joint Requirements Oversight Council. After assessing proposals and coordinating departmentwide participation, the BA FCB then makes recommendations on ISR capability proposals to the Chairman of the Joint Chiefs of Staff in order to assist in the Chairman's task of identifying and assessing the priority of joint capabilities, considering alternatives to acquisition programs, and ensuring that the priority of joint capabilities reflects resource levels projected by the Secretary of Defense.[47]

Despite its coordination role, the BA FCB did not routinely engage in early coordination with sponsors to communicate information necessary to ensure comprehensive and rigorous analysis and to ensure that sponsors were aware of other organizations' and services' existing and developmental ISR capabilities. Our review showed that the BA FCB did not coordinate with five of the seven sponsors while they were conducting their capabilities-based assessments, although Joint Staff policy calls upon the BA FCB to do so in order to promote efficiencies in ISR capability development and to ensure that sponsors' assessments adequately leverage the expertise of the DOD components to identify promising solutions. The five sponsors told us that they coordinated with the BA FCB only after they had submitted their completed ISR capability proposals to the BA FCB. Of the remaining two sponsors, one had minimal interaction with the BA FCB, while the other was in contact with a member of the BA FCB working group while conducting the capabilities-based assessment. Once the BA FCB received copies of these ISR capability proposals, it did facilitate departmentwide participation by serving as a forum where DOD

---

[46] Functional Capabilities Boards may establish one or more working groups to serve as their operational arms in addressing JCIDS and other activities. For more information about working group membership, see Chairman of the Joint Chiefs of Staff Instruction 3137.01C, *The Functional Capabilities Board Process* (Nov. 12, 2004).

[47] Chairman of the Joint Chiefs of Staff Instruction 5123.01C, *Charter of the Joint Requirements Oversight Council* (Nov. 9, 2006).

components formally commented on ISR capability proposals. Sponsors are nevertheless responsible for addressing and resolving these comments. For example, during the commenting process for an Army proposal for a language translation capability, the National Security Agency expressed disagreement, commenting that the Army proposal omitted practical descriptions of how the technology would be achieved and did not address policy and programming issues that it believed were the underlying cause of the capability gap. Thus, although the BA FCB oversaw the commenting process and provided the forum in which this discussion took place, the Army and the National Security Agency resolved their disagreement by revising the proposal with limited Joint Staff involvement.

Furthermore, the BA FCB did not systematically review the quality of the sponsors' capabilities-based assessments. Although the BA FCB is not required by Joint Staff policy and guidance to review the sponsors' capabilities-based assessments, such a review would serve as a means of providing oversight of potential solutions to achieve optimum effectiveness and efficiency—a key BA FCB task. Moreover, the lack of early coordination to ensure the quality of the sponsors' assessments makes the review of the completed assessments an important tool for enhancing capabilities integration and minimizing redundancies. BA FCB members noted that sponsors' analysis can and does take a variety of forms, including studies that were done on related topics but were not initially intended to support the ISR capability proposal. Members of the BA FCB stated that they look for evidence of analysis underpinning the ISR capability proposal, and if analysis has been conducted, they generally consider it sufficient. However, BA FCB officials also told us that they generally do not review sponsors' capabilities-based assessments when evaluating proposals for new ISR capabilities. We found that, of the seven capabilities-based assessments that the sponsors conducted, the BA FCB obtained copies of six, which were proactively provided to them by the sponsors. For the one remaining capabilities-based assessment, the sponsor reported that it did not provide copies of its assessment and the BA FCB did not request them. In addition, the BA FCB did not obtain or systematically review any alternative types of analysis that were used in place of a capabilities-based assessment by the other sponsors that did not conduct capabilities-based assessments. In all of these cases, the BA FCB neither requested copies of the analysis, nor did the sponsor proactively provide its alternative type of analysis.

| DOD's Limited Oversight of the Process for Developing Future ISR Capabilities Is Attributable to Several Factors | The BA FCB did not effectively oversee the process for developing future ISR capabilities by ensuring the implementation of existing guidance related to oversight activities, such as coordination with sponsors and reviews of assessments, for three key reasons. First, the BA FCB has not developed tools to enable systematic review of sponsors' capabilities-based assessments. Specifically, the BA FCB lacks a comprehensive source of information, augmenting the ISR Integration Roadmap, that would identify the full range of existing and developmental ISR capabilities within the ISR enterprise and serve as a tool for assessing the jointness and efficiency of the sponsors' proposed ISR solutions. Although BA FCB officials agreed that knowing the full range of existing and developmental ISR capabilities would be useful in reviewing sponsors' ISR capability proposals, no such complete and up-to-date source of information currently exists. Without readily available information about existing and developmental ISR capabilities, the BA FCB is limited in its ability to systematically review sponsors' capabilities-based assessments to promote cross-service efficiencies in ISR capability development and to conduct oversight of potential solutions to achieve optimum effectiveness and efficiency. Moreover, the majority of the sponsors that conducted assessments said they could not be certain that they had gathered all relevant information to inform their respective assessments, stating that their efforts to obtain information on existing and developmental ISR capabilities were not systematic and often dependent on the use of personal contacts. Some sponsors did take steps to identify existing DOD ISR capabilities when conducting their assessments, such as reviewing a JCIDS database containing other ISR capability proposals and contacting others, both within and outside of their organizations, about potentially related ISR capabilities. Nonetheless, the JCIDS database only contains information on proposals submitted to the Joint Staff, not on existing and developmental ISR capabilities that have been developed and fielded through DOD processes other than JCIDS. In the absence of a comprehensive source of information and early coordination to facilitate the sharing of such information from the BA FCB to the sponsors, sponsors drew from incomplete informational sources when conducting their capabilities-based assessments and sponsors became aware of shortfalls late in the review process. For example, one sponsor said its proposal passed through two levels of Joint Staff review before the sponsor was asked, at the final level of review, whether leveraging a particular technology had been considered as a potential way to fill an identified capability gap; the technology had not been considered because the sponsor was not aware of it. In another case, a request from a high-level Joint Staff official later in the review process resulted in a Navy sponsor and the BA FCB conducting an ad hoc effort, after the |

development of the proposal, to research and develop a list of all DOD's ISR capabilities and demonstrate that a relevant capability gap existed.

Second, the BA FCB does not have the ability to effectively oversee the process for developing future ISR capabilities because there is no monitoring mechanism to ensure that key activities—such as early coordination between sponsors and the BA FCB to facilitate the sharing of information relevant to the sponsors' assessments, and BA FCB review of the assessments—are fully implemented. Standards for internal control in the federal government provide a framework for agencies to achieve effective and efficient operations and ultimately to improve accountability.[48] One of these standards requires that monitoring, such as supervisory activities, should assess the quality of performance over time. Specifically, managers should (1) identify performance gaps by comparing actual performance and achievements to planned results, and (2) determine appropriate adjustments to program management, accountability, and resource allocation in order to improve overall mission accomplishment. To this end, managers should use both ongoing monitoring activities as well as separate evaluations to identify gaps, if any, in performance. Without the development of a monitoring mechanism to ensure implementation of key activities, the BA FCB may not be well-positioned to carry out its oversight of new ISR capabilities as called for by existing Joint Staff guidance.

Third, BA FCB staff said that they lack adequate numbers of dedicated personnel with engineering expertise to engage in early coordination with sponsors and review the capabilities-based assessments that support the ISR capability proposals. For example, BA FCB officials related that they have 12 authorized positions to carry out the BA FCB's responsibilities, but, as of early December 2007, they had 7 assigned personnel—representing a fill rate of 58 percent—with only 4 or 5 of these devoted full-time to BA FCB duties. BA FCB officials also stated that representatives from DOD components who attend BA FCB meetings in order to provide comments on new ISR capability proposals generally do so as a collateral duty, while other components may not send a regularly attending representative. Because the representatives who attend sometimes vary from meeting to meeting and are attending only as a collateral duty, BA FCB officials expressed concern about the ability of

---

[48] GAO, *Standards for Internal Control in the Federal Government*, GAO/AIMD-00-21.3.1 (Washington, D.C.: November 1999).

the BA FCB to most effectively review proposals for new ISR capabilities. Moreover, in addition to reviewing proposals for new ISR capabilities, BA FCB officials have additional responsibilities, such as reviewing other JCIDS documents for ISR capabilities that are in more advanced stages of development[49] and in obtaining feedback from combatant commanders on warfighter needs. Determining the necessary workforce skills and competencies for achieving current and future needs is a key function of workforce planning. Without an assessment of the BA FCB's capabilities to perform its oversight activities related to the review of new ISR capability proposals and coordination with the sponsors, the BA FCB may not be well-positioned to fully carry out the task of promoting efficiencies in ISR capability development.

Furthermore, Joint Staff officials stated that although the BA FCB has coordination and oversight responsibilities, it lacks the ability to correct stovepiped efforts that it identifies through the JCIDS process. For example, BA FCB officials described a recent case in which two proposals for similar environmental capabilities were submitted to the BA FCB by different sponsors. However, the BA FCB does not have the ability to require these two sponsors to work together on their respective capability proposals or to combine them, according to Joint Staff officials. Despite this, a Joint Staff official said the BA FCB is currently coordinating with these sponsors to try to increase efficiencies. The Joint Requirements Oversight Council approved both proposals, while directing the sponsors of each to work with a designated board to examine ways to make the programs more efficient, such as combining them. In addition, the sponsors have preliminarily agreed to merge their respective ISR programs during the next phase of the acquisition process. We are currently conducting a separate review of the JCIDS process that focuses on the extent to which the process has improved outcomes in weapons system acquisition programs, including structural factors, if any, that affect DOD's ability to prioritize and balance capability needs. We expect our report based on this review to be issued later in 2008.

Since the BA FCB did not conduct key oversight activities, including early coordination with sponsors and review of their assessments, neither the BA FCB nor the sponsors can be assured that the sponsors' assessments

---

[49] For example, as of December 2007, the BA FCB was the primary Functional Capabilities Board for 47 proposals for capabilities already in development, and was the secondary Functional Capabilities Board for 63 proposals for capabilities already in development.

have considered the full range of potential joint solutions to minimize inefficiency and redundancy in ISR capability development—a key aim of the JCIDS process. Moreover, without a readily available source of information about all existing and developmental ISR capabilities that might potentially fill a gap, the BA FCB and the sponsors lack a tool to facilitate departmentwide efficiencies when reviewing proposed ISR capabilities. Accordingly, the process for developing future ISR capabilities may not ensure identification of joint solutions for requirements. The BA FCB recommendations inform which ISR capability proposals are ultimately approved by the Chairman of the Joint Chiefs of Staff as being essential to DOD's ability to fight and win future wars. After the Chairman approves ISR capability proposals, the military services and DOD organizations may begin the process of developing and acquiring the systems that deliver the validated capability. The systems, once acquired, will likely deliver capabilities not only to the warfighter, but also to the broader national intelligence community. Without effective oversight of ISR capability development, efficient solutions are likely to go unidentified, while new programs continue to move through development without sufficient knowledge, potentially resulting in unnecessary investment or cost increases and schedule delays further in the acquisition process that affect the entire ISR enterprise. As sponsors of proposed ISR capabilities each currently plan unique solutions to their similar needs, oversight is key to achieving efficiencies among proposed ISR capabilities at the outset of the capability development process.

Conclusions

Congress and DOD have consistently emphasized the importance of DOD integrating its ISR activities across the defense and national intelligence components of the ISR enterprise. Increased integration of the ISR enterprise would help minimize capability redundancies and gaps and maximize capability effectiveness by improving communication across the defense and intelligence communities to leverage common investments for common missions. Although DOD has taken steps to improve the integration of ISR investments—such as by issuing the ISR Integration Roadmap and managing a departmentwide portfolio of ISR capabilities— these initiatives do not provide ISR decision makers with a clear vision of a future ISR enterprise and a unified investment approach to achieve that vision. Without a clear vision and a unified investment approach, ISR decision makers lack the key management tools they need to comprehensively identify what ISR investments DOD needs to make to achieve its strategic goals, evaluate tradeoffs between competing needs, and assess progress in achieving strategic goals. Thus, USD(I) and other senior DOD officials are not well-positioned to meet future ISR needs in a more integrated manner by exerting discipline over ISR spending to ensure progress toward strategic goals. Moreover, a long-term vision of a future ISR enterprise, consisting of a well-defined target architecture that depicts what ISR capabilities are needed to support strategic goals, would be useful not only to ISR decision makers evaluating tradeoffs between competing needs but also to sponsors developing proposals for new ISR capabilities. Without readily available information on existing and developmental ISR capabilities to assist the sponsors in developing the assessments and the BA FCB in reviewing them, neither the sponsors nor the BA FCB can be assured that these assessments have considered the full range of potential joint solutions to minimize inefficiency and redundancy in ISR capability development. Further, without a monitoring mechanism to ensure implementation of Joint Staff policy calling for early coordination between the BA FCB and the sponsors and for completion of capabilities-based assessments, the Joint Requirements Oversight Council may not receive complete assessments to support its decisions about the most efficient and effective proposed ISR capabilities to meet defense and national intelligence needs. Additionally, without consistent early coordination and thorough reviews of assessments, sponsors participating in DOD's requirements identification process may not have an incentive to conduct thorough assessments and may focus their proposals on their individual needs without fully ensuring identification of joint solutions for requirements. Finally, without a needs assessment that reviews the BA FCB's staffing levels, expertise, and workload to engage in early coordination with sponsors and review capabilities-based assessments and a plan, if needed, that addresses any identified shortfalls, the BA FCB may not be well-positioned to conduct oversight of potential ISR solutions to achieve optimum effectiveness and efficiency. Thus, DOD cannot be assured that it is developing the optimal mix of ISR capabilities to achieve its goals of better integrating the ISR enterprise.

Recommendations for Executive Action

We recommend the Secretary of Defense take the following four actions:

- Direct the Under Secretary of Defense for Intelligence to develop a vision of a future ISR architecture that addresses a longer period of time than the 5-year ISR budget and is based on an independent analysis of expected future requirements and strategic goals. This architecture should be sufficiently detailed to inform a comprehensive assessment and prioritization of capability gaps and overlaps, to allow decision makers to evaluate tradeoffs between competing needs, and to assess progress in addressing capability gaps and overlaps in order to achieve ISR strategic goals.

- Direct the Chairman of the Joint Chiefs of Staff and the Under Secretary of Defense for Intelligence to collaborate, with one of these organizations assigned as the lead, in developing a comprehensive source of information, which augments the ISR Integration Roadmap, on all existing and developmental ISR capabilities throughout the ISR enterprise for sponsors to use in conducting capabilities-based assessments and for the Battlespace Awareness Functional Capabilities Board to use in evaluating them.

- Direct the Chairman of the Joint Chiefs of Staff to develop a supervisory review or other monitoring mechanism to ensure that (1) the Battlespace Awareness Functional Capabilities Board and the sponsors engage in early coordination to facilitate sponsors' consideration of existing and developmental ISR capabilities in developing their capabilities-based assessments, (2) capabilities-based assessments are completed, and (3) the Battlespace Awareness Functional Capabilities Board uses systematic procedures for reviewing the assessments.

- Direct the Chairman of the Joint Chiefs of Staff to (1) review the Battlespace Awareness Functional Capabilities Board's staffing levels and expertise and workload to engage in early coordination with sponsors and review capabilities-based assessments, and (2) if shortfalls are identified, develop a plan that addresses any identified shortfalls of personnel, resources, or training, assigns responsibility for actions, and establishes time frames for implementing the plan.

Agency Comments and Our Evaluation

We provided a draft of this report to DOD and the Office of the Director of National Intelligence. DOD provided written comments, in which it agreed or partially agreed with three recommendations and disagreed with one recommendation. DOD's comments are reprinted in their entirety in appendix II.[50] In addition, both DOD and the Office of the Director of National Intelligence provided technical comments, which we have incorporated into the report as appropriate.

DOD agreed with our recommendation to develop a vision of a future ISR architecture that addresses a longer period of time than the 5-year ISR

---

[50] In its written comments, DOD divided our four recommendations into seven recommendations, commenting upon each separately. In our evaluation, we discuss DOD's comments in the context of our four final recommendations.

budget and is based on an independent analysis of expected future requirements and strategic goals. The department stated that work is underway to develop a future ISR architecture, including a plan of action and milestones.

DOD partially agreed with our recommendation to develop a comprehensive source of information on existing and developmental ISR capabilities. In its written comments, DOD agreed that such a source of information is needed to augment the ISR Integration Roadmap. However, DOD stated that the task of developing this comprehensive source of information to facilitate the identification of all capabilities throughout the ISR enterprise should be assigned to the Under Secretary of Defense for Intelligence, as the Battlespace Awareness Capability Portfolio Manager, rather than the Joint Staff as we recommended. We originally recommended that this task be directed to the Joint Staff because the need for such a comprehensive source of information was most evident in the difficulties in developing and reviewing ISR capability proposals as called for under the JCIDS review process, which is managed by the Joint Staff. We agree with DOD that the Under Secretary of Defense for Intelligence, who is responsible for both developing the ISR Integration Roadmap and leading the Battlespace Awareness capability portfolio management effort, is a key player in efforts to improve integration of future joint ISR capabilities and could be logically assigned leadership responsibilities for this task. We have modified this recommendation in the final report to clarify that the Secretary of Defense could assign leadership to either organization, in consultation with the other, to develop the comprehensive source of information that sponsors and the BA FCB need. In the draft report, we had included in this recommendation two actions that the Joint Staff could take to improve the process for identifying future ISR capabilities. In modifying this recommendation to reflect DOD's comment that the Under Secretary of Defense for Intelligence could have the lead role in developing the information source, we moved these two actions to our third recommendation, thereby consolidating actions that the Joint Staff needs to take into one recommendation that considers key responsibilities within the JCIDS process.

DOD partially agreed with our recommendation related to the need to ensure that (1) the Battlespace Awareness Functional Capabilities Board and the sponsors engage in early coordination to facilitate sponsors' consideration of existing and developmental ISR capabilities in developing their capabilities-based assessments, (2) capabilities-based assessments are completed, and (3) the Battlespace Awareness Functional Capabilities Board uses systematic procedures for reviewing the assessments. In its written comments, DOD agreed that all three elements of this recommendation are needed but stated that changes in guidance were not needed. Our recommendation did not specifically call for additional guidance but was focused on the need to execute existing guidance. For example, as the report describes, Joint Staff policy calls for the sponsors and Functional Capabilities Board to work together during the analysis process, but the sponsors of the proposals we reviewed and the BA FCB did not consistently engage in this coordination. In addition, although Joint Staff policy gives the BA FCB responsibility for providing oversight of potential solutions to achieve optimum effectiveness and efficiency in ISR capability development, we found that the BA FCB did not systematically review capabilities-based assessments as a means of providing such oversight. In response to DOD's comments, we modified this recommendation to clarify that DOD should ensure compliance with its existing guidance by developing a monitoring mechanism that would ensure that early coordination takes place and that capabilities-based assessments are completed and reviewed. In its comments, the department also stated that our report is misleading because we evaluated some programs initiated prior to the genesis of JCIDS. As our report describes, the scope of our review included 19 ISR capability proposals that were introduced only after the implementation of JCIDS in 2003. We noted that some of these proposals used analysis conducted prior to the implementation of JCIDS as a substitute for the capabilities-based assessment that is required by the JCIDS process. However, we were unable to apply JCIDS criteria to evaluate them because these proposals did not have capabilities-based assessments. In addition, our recommendation to ensure that capabilities-based assessments are completed was based on our observations of all 19 ISR capability proposals, including not only the 12 proposals that lacked capabilities-based assessments but also the 7 proposals whose assessments varied in rigor and completeness.

DOD disagreed with our recommendation that the department (1) review the BA FCB's staffing levels and expertise and workload to engage in early coordination with sponsors and review capabilities-based assessments, and (2) if shortfalls of personnel, resources, or training needed are identified, develop a plan to address them, including assigning responsibility for actions and establishing time frames for implementing the plan. In its written comments, the department stated that Joint Staff policy clearly defines the roles and responsibilities of the sponsors and Functional Capabilities Boards. We agree that Joint Staff policy defines roles and responsibilities of these groups, and we note that this policy assigns responsibility to both the sponsors and the Functional Capabilities

Board to coordinate with each other. We did not recommend that further policy direction was needed, as DOD stated in its comments. DOD also noted that it had conducted a review of Functional Capabilities Board personnel and resources in fiscal year 2007, which did not identify deficiencies. However, workload issues and lack of technical skills among staff were mentioned to us by defense officials as reasons why early coordination and reviews were not being systematically performed as part of the BA FCB's oversight function—a key function called for in Joint Staff policy. Therefore, in light of our finding that the BA FCB did not fully implement these key oversight activities, we continue to believe that the department should reconsider whether the BA FCB has the appropriate number of staff with the appropriate skills to fully implement these oversight activities.

As agreed with your offices, unless you publicly announce its contents earlier, we plan no further distribution of this report until 30 days from its date. At that time, we will send copies of this report to interested congressional committees; the Secretary of Defense; the Under Secretary of Defense for Intelligence; the Chairman of the Joint Chiefs of Staff; the Secretaries of the Army, Navy, and Air Force; the Commandant of the Marine Corps; the Office of the Director of National Intelligence; and the Director, Office of Management and Budget. We will also make copies available to others upon request. In addition, this report is available at no charge on the GAO Web site at http://www.gao.gov.

If you or your staff have any questions about this report, please contact me at (202) 512-5431 or dagostinod@gao.gov. Contact points for our Offices of Congressional Relations and Public Affairs may be found on the last page of this report. GAO staff who made key contributions to this report are listed in appendix III.

Sincerely,

Davi M. D'Agostino
Director, Defense Capabilities and Management

Appendix I: Scope and Methodology

To describe the challenges, if any, that the Department of Defense (DOD) faces in working to achieve an integrated ISR enterprise, we reviewed documents on the operation of DOD's ISR enterprise and the national intelligence community and discussed the ISR enterprise and its complexities with a variety of defense-related intelligence organizations, as well as with the Office of the Director of National Intelligence. Specifically, we discussed coordination challenges faced by components of DOD's ISR enterprise with officials from the Office of the Under Secretary of Defense for Intelligence, Arlington, VA; the Joint Staff, Arlington, Va.; the National Security Space Office, Fairfax, Va.; U.S. Strategic Command's Joint Functional Component Command for ISR, Washington, D.C.; the Defense Intelligence Agency, Washington, D.C.; the National Geospatial-Intelligence Agency, Reston, Va.; and the National Security Agency, Annapolis Junction, Md.; and the Office of the Director of National Intelligence, Washington, D.C.

To assess DOD's management approach for improving integration of future ISR investments, we reviewed DOD's ISR Integration Roadmap and other ISR integration efforts within DOD. We compared DOD's ISR Integration Roadmap to key elements of an enterprise architecture to determine whether the Roadmap, in whole or in part, met these key elements. We identified these key elements by reviewing DOD and federal guidance on enterprise architecture best practices, specifically the Department of Defense Architecture Framework and the Chief Information Officer Council's Practical Guide to Federal Enterprise Architecture. In addition, we reviewed the implementation of the Battlespace Awareness capability portfolio management test case led by the Office of the Under Secretary of Defense for Intelligence. We compared these efforts to portfolio management best practices we identified by reviewing our past work on this subject. We also obtained information from and discussed DOD's ISR Integration Roadmap and DOD ISR integration efforts and challenges with senior officials from the Office of the Secretary of Defense, Arlington, Va.; the Joint Staff, Arlington, Va.; the Office of the Under Secretary of Defense for Intelligence, Arlington, Va.; the Office of the Assistant Secretary of Defense for Networks and Information Integration, Arlington, Va.; the National Security Space Office, Fairfax, Va.; U.S. Strategic Command's Joint Functional Component Command for ISR, Washington, D.C.; the Defense Intelligence Agency, Washington, D.C.; and the Office of the Director of National Intelligence, Washington, D.C.

To evaluate the extent to which DOD has implemented key activities within the Joint Capabilities Integration and Development System (JCIDS) to ensure that proposed new ISR capabilities fill gaps, are not duplicative, and use a joint approach to filling warfighters' needs based on a thorough analysis of existing capabilities, we identified 19 ISR capability proposals, described in table 1, that were submitted to the Joint Staff since the implementation of JCIDS in 2003 and for which the Battlespace Awareness Functional Capabilities Board was designated the lead Functional Capabilities Board. In total, there were 20 ISR capability proposals that met these criteria; however, 1 of the 20 proposals, along with its underlying capabilities-based assessment, was highly classified and, since we did not have the appropriate security clearances, we did not review this proposal. For the remaining 19 ISR capability proposals, we evaluated the extent to which they were generated and validated in accordance with Joint Staff policies and procedures.

Table 1: ISR Capability Proposals Submitted to the Joint Staff Since the Implementation of JCIDS in 2003 and for Which the Battlespace Awareness Functional Capabilities Board was Designated the Lead

Capability title	Sponsor
Advanced Distributed Aperture Sensor System	U.S. Special Operations Command
Airborne Overhead Cooperative Operations	U.S. Joint Forces Command
Expeditionary Delivery of Airborne Full Motion Video	Air Force
Full Spectrum Intelligence	Navy
Joint Spectral	National Geospatial-Intelligence Agency
Joint Tier II Unmanned Aircraft System	Marine Corps
Littoral Battlespace Sensing, Fusion, and Integration	Navy
Marine Corps Intelligence, Surveillance, Reconnaissance Enterprise	Marine Corps
National Signatures Program	Defense Intelligence Agency
Rapid Attack Identification, Detection, and Reporting System	Air Force
Sequoyah Foreign Language Translation System	Army
Small Unmanned Solutions	U.S. Air Force Special Operations Command
Space Based Space Surveillance	Air Force
Space Fence	Air Force
Space Radar Program	Air Force
Space Test and Training Range	Air Force
Universal Phase History Data	National Geospatial-Intelligence Agency
Vertical Unmanned Aerial Vehicle	Marine Corps
Weapons and Space FIS Modernization	National Security Agency

Source: GAO analysis of sponsor data accessed via the Joint Staff's Knowledge Management/Decision Support system.

Specifically, for each of the 19 capability proposals, we obtained
capabilities-based assessments or other JCIDS analysis documents that
were produced by sponsors of these ISR capability proposals, and we
performed a dependent document review of the 7 ISR capability proposals
that included a capabilities-based assessment, using a data collection
instrument based on applicable versions of the Chairman of the Joint
Chiefs of Staff Instruction 3170.01, *Joint Capabilities Integration and
Development System.* In conducting this document review, we considered
whether these JCIDS analysis documents showed evidence of the
following elements: (1) a full review conducted, (2) cost information
included, (3) consideration of the full range of existing and developmental
stage ISR assets, (4) consideration of modifications as potential solutions,
and (5) consideration of potential redundancies. The results of this
analysis are shown in figure 5 of this report. Our specific methodology for
this analysis is as follows:

- To determine whether a full review had been conducted, we
  determined whether a Functional Needs Analysis (FNA) and
  Functional Solution Analysis (FSA) existed and whether they flowed
  from a Functional Area Analysis (FAA) and FNA, respectively. As
  generally described in Joint Staff guidance, an FAA identifies the
  operational tasks, conditions, and standards needed to achieve military
  objectives. An FNA assesses the ability of current and planned systems
  to deliver the capabilities and tasks identified in the FAA in order to
  produce a list of capability gaps and identify redundancies. An FSA will
  identify joint approaches to fill the identified capability gaps.

- To determine whether cost information was included, we reviewed
  whether the FSA considered costs of the proposed solutions. As
  generally described in Joint Staff guidance, the FSA analysis must
  evaluate the cost to develop and procure materiel approaches
  compared to the cost of sustaining an existing capability.

- To determine whether the full range of existing and developmental-
  stage ISR assets was considered, we reviewed whether the FSA
  considered interagency or foreign materiel solutions and whether the
  FNA or FSA considered the full range of joint solutions. We defined the
  full range of joint solutions as including strategic, operational, and
  tactical ISR assets as well as developing or recently developed ISR
  systems. As generally described in Joint Staff policy, the FNA assesses
  the entire range of doctrine, organization, training, materiel, logistics,
  personnel, and facilities and policy as an inherent part of defining
  capability needs, and the FSA assesses all potential materiel and non-
  materiel ways to fill capability gaps as identified by the FNA, including

changes that leverage existing materiel capabilities, product improvements, and adoption of interagency or foreign materiel solutions.

- To determine whether modifications were considered as potential solutions, we reviewed whether the FSA considered using existing systems differently or modifying policies and processes. As generally described in Joint Staff guidance, the FSA is to identify combinations of materiel and non-materiel approaches and examine additional approaches by conducting market research to determine whether commercial or non-developmental items are available or could be modified to meet the desired capability.

- To determine whether potential redundancies were considered, we reviewed whether either the FNA or the FSA identified potentially redundant ISR capabilities. As generally described in Joint Staff guidance, an FNA should describe a capability overlap by comparing desired functions with current capabilities. However, we considered the capabilities-based assessment as having identified potential redundancies if such redundancies were included in either the FNA or FSA.

We identified the above elements by analyzing current and superseded versions of the Joint Staff instruction on the JCIDS process—specifically, the Chairman of the Joint Chiefs of Staff Instruction 3170.01, *Joint Capabilities Integration and Development System*—to determine the changes over time and the criteria common to all versions. Further, we reviewed the following policies and procedures related to the validation of ISR capabilities through JCIDS: Chairman of the Joint Chiefs of Staff Instruction 5123.01, *Charter of the Joint Requirements Oversight Council*; Chairman of the Joint Chiefs of Staff Instruction 3137.01, *The Functional Capabilities Board Process*; Chairman of the Joint Chiefs of Staff Instruction 3170.01, *Joint Capabilities Integration and Development System*; and Chairman of the Joint Chiefs of Staff Manual 3170.01, *Operation of the Joint Capabilities Integration and Development System*. In order to conduct this review of JCIDS policies and procedures, we included in our scope the current and superseded versions of these guidance documents; accordingly, we reviewed all instructions and manuals relevant to DOD's JCIDS process that were in effect at some point between the publication of the initial JCIDS instruction (Joint Chiefs of Staff Instruction 3170.01A, dated June 24, 2003) and the conclusion of our review (March 2008).[1] In addition, we obtained insight into the procedures and challenges associated with validating proposals for new ISR capabilities through discussions with officials from the Office of the Under Secretary of Defense for Intelligence, Arlington, Va.; the Joint Staff, Arlington, Va.; the Battlespace Awareness Functional Capabilities Board, Arlington, Va.; and the sponsors of the 19 ISR capability proposals that we reviewed. The sponsors with whom we spoke were officials from the Air Force; Army; Navy; Marine Corps; U.S. Special Operations Command; U.S. Joint Forces Command; Defense Intelligence Agency; National Geospatial-Intelligence Agency; and National Security Agency.

---

[1] Specifically, we reviewed the following: Chairman of the Joint Chiefs of Staff Instruction 5123.01A, *Charter of the Joint Requirements Oversight Council* (Mar. 8, 2001); Chairman of the Joint Chiefs of Staff Instruction 5123.01B, *Charter of the Joint Requirements Oversight Council* (Apr. 15, 2004); Chairman of the Joint Chiefs of Staff Instruction 5123.01C, *Charter of the Joint Requirements Oversight Council* (Nov. 9, 2006); Chairman of the Joint Chiefs of Staff Instruction 3137.01B, *The Joint Warfighting Capabilities Assessment Process* (Apr. 15, 2002); Chairman of the Joint Chiefs of Staff Instruction 3137.01C, *The Functional Capabilities Board Process* (Nov. 12, 2004); Chairman of the Joint Chiefs of Staff Instruction 3170.01C, *Joint Capabilities Integration and Development System* (June 24, 2003); Chairman of the Joint Chiefs of Staff Instruction 3170.01D, *Joint Capabilities Integration and Development System* (Mar. 12, 2004); Chairman of the Joint Chiefs of Staff Instruction 3170.01E, *Joint Capabilities Integration and Development System* (May 11, 2005); Chairman of the Joint Chiefs of Staff Instruction 3170.01F, *Joint Capabilities Integration and Development System* (May 1, 2007); Chairman of the Joint Chiefs of Staff Manual 3170.01A, *Operation of the Joint Capabilities Integration and Development System* (Mar. 12, 2004); Chairman of the Joint Chiefs of Staff Manual 3170.01B, *Operation of the Joint Capabilities Integration and Development System* (May 11, 2005); and Chairman of the Joint Chiefs of Staff Manual 3170.01C, *Operation of the Joint Capabilities Integration and Development System* (May 1, 2007).

Appendix II: Comments from the Department of Defense

OFFICE OF THE UNDER SECRETARY OF DEFENSE
5000 DEFENSE PENTAGON
WASHINGTON, DC 20301-5000

INTELLIGENCE

FEB 1 5 2008

Ms. Davi M. D'Agostino
Director, Defense Capabilities and Management
U.S. Government Accountability Office
441 G. Street, N.W.
Washington, DC 20548

Dear Ms. D'Agostino:

This is the Department of Defense response to the GAO draft report, GAO-08-374, "INTELLIGENCE, SURVEILLANCE, AND RECONNAISSANCE: DoD Can Better Assess and Integrate ISR Capabilities and Oversee Development of Future ISR Capabilities," dated January 17, 2008, (GAO Code 351027).

DoD appreciates the opportunity to review and comment on the draft report. Detailed comments on the GAO recommendations and technical comments are enclosed. For further questions concerning this report please contact my action officer, Colonel Cordell DeLaPena, Director, Unmanned Aircraft Systems, (703) 607-0427.

Sincerely,

Betty J. Sapp
Under Secretary of Defense for Intelligence
(Acquisition, Resources, and Technology)

Enclosures:
1. DoD Response to Recommendations
2. DoD Technical Comments

GAO DRAFT REPORT – DATED JANUARY 17, 2008
GAO CODE 351027 /GAO-08-374

"INTELLIGENCE, SURVEILLANCE, AND RECONNAISSANCE: DoD Can Better Assess
and Integrate ISR Capabilities and Oversee Development of Future ISR Capabilities"

DEPARTMENT OF DEFENSE COMMENTS
TO THE RECOMMENDATIONS

RECOMMENDATION 1: The GAO recommends that the Secretary of Defense direct the
Under Secretary of Defense for Intelligence to develop a vision of a future intelligence,
surveillance, and reconnaissance (ISR) architecture that addresses a longer period of time than
the 5-year ISR budget and is based on an independent analysis of expected future requirements
and strategic goals. This architecture should be sufficiently detailed to inform a comprehensive
assessment and prioritization of capability gaps and overlaps, to allow decision makers to
evaluate competing needs, and to assess progress in addressing capability gaps and overlaps in
order to achieve ISR strategic goals.

DOD RESPONSE: Concur. Work is underway to develop a vision of a future intelligence,
surveillance, and reconnaissance (ISR) architecture that addresses a longer period of time than
the 5-year ISR budget and is based on an independent analysis of expected future requirements
and strategic goals. The plan of action and milestones for this effort are being developed now
and should be finalized by the end of February 2008.

RECOMMENDATION 2: The GAO recommends that the Secretary of Defense direct the
Chairman of the Joint Chiefs of Staff, in consultation with the Under Secretary of Defense for
Intelligence, to develop a comprehensive source of information that augments the Intelligence,
Surveillance, and Reconnaissance (ISR) Integration Roadmap to facilitate the identification of
all capabilities throughout the ISR enterprise–including all existing and developmental ISR
capabilities–in order to assist the sponsors in conducting capabilities-based assessments and the
Battlespace Awareness Functional Capabilities Board in evaluating them.

DOD RESPONSE: Partially Concur. We concur with the need to develop a comprehensive
source of information to augment the intelligence, surveillance, and reconnaissance (ISR)
Integration Roadmap. However, this task is directly related to the development of the future
ISR architecture and is more appropriately tasked to the Battlespace Awareness Capability
Portfolio Manager rather than the Chairman of the Joint Chiefs of Staff.

RECOMMENDATION 3: The GAO recommends that the Secretary of Defense direct the
Chairman of the Joint Chiefs of Staff, in consultation with the Under Secretary of Defense for
Intelligence, to ensure that capabilities-based assessments are completed.

1

DOD RESPONSE: Partially Concur. The Department agrees that Capability Based Assessments (CBA) should be completed; however, the Joint Staff disagrees with the assertion that additional direction is required. CJCSM 3170.01C "Operation of the Joint Capabilities Integration and Development System (JCIDS)" provides clear guidance on the necessity and process for completing capability-based assessments. The GAO's review is misleading. The review evaluated many programs initiated prior to the genesis of JCIDS. Five of the ten programs identified as not having a formal CBA are considered as having been based on pre-JCIDS analysis. In these specific cases, prior analysis was reviewed and accepted as sufficient if it was deemed to meet the needs of the Joint Requirements Oversight Council (JROC). This exemption was structured to avoid forcing programs to reaccomplish previously completed analysis unless there was a compelling need to do so.

RECOMMENDATION 4: The GAO recommends that the Secretary of Defense direct the Chairman of the Joint Chiefs of Staff, in consultation with the Under Secretary of Defense for Intelligence, to develop systematic procedures for reviewing the capabilities-based assessments.

DOD RESPONSE: Partially concur. The Department agrees with the need for systematic procedures for reviewing capabilities-based assessments; however, we disagree with the assertion that additional direction is required. CJCSM 3170.01C already contains a checklist for reviewing capabilities based assessment. Each element, Functional Area Analysis, Functional Needs Analysis and Functional Solutions Analysis has a defined set of go/no go criteria (see pages A-10 through A-17)

RECOMMENDATION 5: The GAO recommends that the Secretary of Defense direct the Chairman of the Joint Chiefs of Staff to clarify the expectation for the Battlespace Awareness Functional Capabilities Board to engage in early coordination with sponsors to ensure sponsors' ability to access a comprehensive source of information on existing and developmental Intelligence, Surveillance, and Reconnaissance capabilities.

DOD RESPONSE: Partially concur. The Department agrees that there is benefit to sponsors engaging in early coordination with the appropriate Functional Capabilities Boards (FCBs); however, the Department disagrees with the assertion that additional direction is required. CJCSI 3170.01F states it is the sponsor's responsibility as part of the Capability Based Assessments process to "work closely with the appropriate FCBs during the analysis process..." (see page C-4)

RECOMMENDATION 6: The GAO recommends that the Secretary of Defense direct the Chairman of the Joint Chiefs of Staff to identify the Battlespace Awareness Functional Capabilities Board's capabilities to engage in early coordination with sponsors and review capabilities-based assessments, including any shortfalls in personnel, resources, and training needed to perform its mission successfully.

DOD RESPONSE: Non-concur. As previously stated, CJCSI 3170.01F and CJCSI 3170.01C clearly define the sponsors and the Functional Capabilities Boards (FCBs) roles and responsibilities in the Joint Capabilities Integration and Development System (JCIDS) process.

2

Further direction is not required. With regards to shortfalls in personnel, resources and training, the Joint Staff conducted an FY07 review of FCB personnel and resources and did not identify any deficiencies. In the area of training, the Joint Staff has already established a new, mandatory training course for all 'Requirements Managers' that will certify them in the writing, reviewing, development, and approval of requirements for Major Defense Acquisition Programs.

RECOMMENDATION 7: The GAO recommends that the Secretary of Defense direct the Chairman of the Joint Chiefs of Staff to develop a plan that addresses any identified shortfalls of personnel, resources, and training; assigns responsibility for actions; and establishes time frames for implementing the plan.

DOD RESPONSE: Non-concur. This recommendation presupposes shortfalls exist in the FCB's personnel, resources, and training. As previously stated, the Joint Staff conducted an FY07 review of functional capabilities board personnel and resources and did not identify any deficiencies. In the area of training, the Joint Staff has already established a new, mandatory training course for all 'Requirements Managers' that will certify them in the writing, reviewing, development, and approval of requirements for Major Defense Acquisition Programs.

3

GAO DRAFT REPORT - DATED January 17, 2008
GAO CODE 351027/GAO-08-374

"INTELLIGENCE, SURVEILLANCE, AND RECONNAISSANCE: DoD Can Better
Assess and Integrate ISR Capabilities and Oversee Development of Future ISR
Capabilities"

DEPARTMENT OF DEFENSE TECHNICAL COMMENTS
ON THE DRAFT REPORT

Page 36, Figure 4.

RECOMMENDATION: Add a note to the timeline figure stating that the chronology
reflects the date on the latest version of the Initial Capabilities Document (ICD) available
to the authors, as earlier versions of some of the documents were staffed at earlier dates
when approved, and required Joint Capabilities Integration and Development System
(JCIDS) analysis steps had not been fully defined. Rationale: The timeline reflects a
mid-2006 entry for the Small Unmanned Solutions ICD, yet the ICD actually entered the
Joint Capabilities Integration and Development System (JCIDS) in mid-2005, before
JCIDS required analysis steps had been fully defined.

Appendix III: GAO Contact and Staff Acknowledgments

GAO Contact	Davi M. D'Agostino, (202) 512-5431 or dagostinod@gao.gov
Acknowledgments	In addition to the contact named above, Margaret G. Morgan, Assistant Director; Catherine H. Brown; Gabrielle A. Carrington; Frank Cristinzio; Grace Coleman; Jay Smale; and Karen Thornton made key contributions to this report.

GAO's Mission	The Government Accountability Office, the audit, evaluation, and investigative arm of Congress, exists to support Congress in meeting its constitutional responsibilities and to help improve the performance and accountability of the federal government for the American people. GAO examines the use of public funds; evaluates federal programs and policies; and provides analyses, recommendations, and other assistance to help Congress make informed oversight, policy, and funding decisions. GAO's commitment to good government is reflected in its core values of accountability, integrity, and reliability.
Obtaining Copies of GAO Reports and Testimony	The fastest and easiest way to obtain copies of GAO documents at no cost is through GAO's Web site (www.gao.gov). Each weekday, GAO posts newly released reports, testimony, and correspondence on its Web site. To have GAO e-mail you a list of newly posted products every afternoon, go to www.gao.gov and select "E-mail Updates."

Order by Mail or Phone	The first copy of each printed report is free. Additional copies are $2 each. A check or money order should be made out to the Superintendent of Documents. GAO also accepts VISA and Mastercard. Orders for 100 or more copies mailed to a single address are discounted 25 percent. Orders should be sent to:
	
	U.S. Government Accountability Office
	441 G Street NW, Room LM
	Washington, DC 20548
	
	To order by Phone: Voice: (202) 512-6000
	                          TDD: (202) 512-2537
	                          Fax: (202) 512-6061

To Report Fraud, Waste, and Abuse in Federal Programs	Contact: Web site: www.gao.gov/fraudnet/fraudnet.htm E-mail: fraudnet@gao.gov Automated answering system: (800) 424-5454 or (202) 512-7470
Congressional Relations	Ralph Dawn, Managing Director, dawnr@gao.gov, (202) 512-4400 U.S. Government Accountability Office, 441 G Street NW, Room 7125 Washington, DC 20548
Public Affairs	Chuck Young, Managing Director, youngc1@gao.gov, (202) 512-4800 U.S. Government Accountability Office, 441 G Street NW, Room 7149 Washington, DC 20548

CPSIA information can be obtained at www.ICGtesting.com
Printed in the USA
LVOW03s1955071015

457329LV00015B/350/P